PRAISE FOR
DEFINE YOURSELF

"I met Aaron in 2017 through our mutual connection and passion for franchising. Since then, I've had the fortune to witness KX grow, evolve, navigate a leadership transition, survive a once in a lifetime pandemic, and continue to thrive. I have huge admiration for the business and the brand that Aaron has built with his team and franchisees. I'm also a big fan of the product. As I'm an endurance athlete prone to injuries, KX has been a game changer for my fitness. Aaron's candid and entertaining account of how the business was founded and has grown is a great case study on what it takes to build a successful franchise operation. I am confident there are many more chapters still to be written in this great story."

DAVID CHRISTIE, Joint CEO, Bakers Delight

"Aaron's story is a great reminder that business is a journey. It's hard, but, by being your authentic self, it can be the most rewarding journey of your life. This book delivers an open, honest and fun reminder for existing business owners, as well as a great insight to new entrepreneurs in an easy, enjoyable, lighthearted read."

JEREMY DYER, Managing Director, Total Fitouts

"Aaron, what a read! A warts-and-all depiction of the amazing journey of the KX brand. Your self-motivation and drive is inspiring. I love that you still have your first ever KX sign. I can't wait to read what your next chapter has in store."

MELANIE GLEESON, Founder & CEO, Endota Spa

"I first met Aaron in 2010 when he had just one KX Studio. I knew straight away he was a real entrepreneur. Watching him grow the KX network from one studio to 100+ studios and over $60 million in annual revenue has been a meteoric rise. Now, he's captured invaluable truths behind building a successful company in *Define Yourself*. Treat this as a blueprint that you can follow."

JACK DELOSA, Founder, The Entourage

"Aaron's passion for movement, health, and entrepreneurship really shines through in this book. He is refreshingly transparent with what has worked and what hasn't. I highly recommend that anyone looking into franchising a business or the business of scalable Pilates begin the process by reading this book."

KEN ENDELMAN, Founder & CEO, Balanced Body

"*Define Yourself* is one of the most inspirational and honest reviews on what it takes to go from idea formation, to true hard graft, through challenges and ultimately to success. Aaron's story is truly inspirational and should form a staple diet in anyone's bookshelf for how to change your life, see opportunity and then work bloody hard to make it happen. I could not recommend this highly enough, especially to those in the health and fitness sector."

GLENN WITHERS, Cofounder & CEO, APPI Health Group

"I've known Aaron since he opened studio number one in 2010 to celebrating KX's ten years on the super yacht on the Sydney Harbour just before COVID, so I have been close to the KX business for quite a while, and it's no surprise that KX has become an inspiring success story.

When you talk to Aaron, you can feel his passion and love for KX and the people within it. Aaron has this incredible ability to have a vision (which grows significantly every year), break it into clear goals, and have the discipline and grit to turn that into a reality. The perfect blend of passion, discipline and a level head that's needed to be an entrepreneur. Chatting with Aaron, there's always some insight to gain and a story to tell. He's crammed in a few average lifetimes already!

Aaron's values and personality shine throughout the KX business, having created a passionate, disciplined, purpose-driven, no-egos culture within KX, reflecting Aaron himself and undoubtedly driving more success. It was impressive to witness the entire KX family rally and persist through the tough last few years of COVID interruptions. Watching them make rapid adjustments and stay positive, all whilst riding the business roller coaster and coming out the other side is a testament to the culture Aaron started and the outstanding leadership of the whole team at KX.

Aaron's knack for absorbing advice, picking out the best learnings from his mentors, friends, and business partners and applying it in his unique way is very impressive and serves him and the KX family well. I've learned much from Aaron and feel privileged to have a front row seat to the journey ahead."

ROSS FASTUCA, CEO & Cofounder, Locomote

"As a business owner at a critical crossroad in my business, I found *Define Yourself* not only highly informative but also very inspirational. An unexpected added bonus is that I have joined KX Pilates to also improve my own fitness levels, something I never considered doing before!"

IAN PUTTKAMMER, Cofounder & CEO, Happy Pops

"Aaron has written an informative and entertaining book with candor and good Aussie humor. His love for family, fitness and franchising shines through as he shares his personal and business journey in building the KX Pilates franchise network, and the experiences that have shaped his thinking as a successful entrepreneur and franchise founder. This is a great book for anyone wanting to succeed in business, especially in the franchising sector as a franchisee or franchisor. Those interested in personal fitness and wellbeing will also get great value from Aaron's insights."

GREG NATHAN, Author of *Profitable Partnerships* & Founder, Franchise Relationships Institute

"I had the pleasure of meeting Aaron in person in 2019. What struck me initially was that he knew exactly who he was, and it was clear that he had a defined purpose in life. This shines through not only in this book but also through all levels of the KX Brand. *Define Yourself* is a journey that really resonated with me as a founder of a business. The key word here is that it is a journey. Aaron has been able to harness the lessons from his successes, challenges and failures and embrace feedback, both internally and externally, with a singular goal to continue to improve the product to be the market leader in this space and provide exceptional member experiences and outcomes.

Aaron is a purpose-driven leader, and his life experiences and business lessons are a good read for any aspiring entrepreneur who is looking to get an idea off the ground and pursue their passion. Similarly, for those that may already be on their own journey and are experiencing the challenges and highs and lows of a start-up, you will get great comfort and insight through Aaron's many learnings that he shares in this book."

CAM FALLOON, Founder, Body Fit Training (BFT)

"*Define Yourself* is a must-read for anyone interested in entrepreneurship. Aaron shares his journey, from discovering Pilates to building a successful global franchise, and shows that the road to success is full of unexpected twists and turns. He highlights the power of determination and hard work and shares valuable insights on franchising and the importance of travel to broaden your worldview. The book is honest, inspiring and full of valuable lessons."

TIM WEST, Founder, UBX Boxing + Strength

DEFINE YOURSELF

DEFINE YOURSELF

When Passion, Purpose and Business Collide

AARON SMITH
Founder of KX Pilates

First published in 2023 by Dean Publishing
PO Box 119,
Mt. Macedon, Victoria, 3441
Australia
deanpublishing.com

DEAN PUBLISHING

Cataloguing-in-Publication Data
National Library of Australia
Title: Define Yourself: When Passion, Purpose and Business Collide
Edition: 1st edn
ISBN: 978-1-925452-64-8
Category: BUSINESS/Franchises/Entrepreneurship/Health and Fitness Industry

Image on page 33 © I C Rapoport / Contributor / Getty Image

DEDICATION

To Andi—my wife, life and business partner. My adventure buddy.
The mother to our three beautiful children. You truly are the secret
behind KX's success. No one will ever know how hard you have worked
and what you have sacrificed to help push KX to where it is today,
and I've never recognized nor thanked you enough.
Thank you for everything.

TABLE OF CONTENTS

PART ONE

HOW IT ALL BEGAN

"Everybody has
to start somewhere.
You have your whole
future ahead of you.
Perfection doesn't
happen right away."

—Haruki Murakami

Chapter 1

LIFE'S TOO SHORT TO BE NORMAL

Sunday mass was a ritual for my big Catholic family, and thanking the Lord by saying grace at the dinner table every night was the norm.

I was the youngest of five kids, with two older sisters and brothers. My two eldest sisters (thirteen and eleven years older than me) were brought up under our parents' strict household rules. By the time I hit my teenage years, with my older brothers' help, my parents had eased their rules, and I had a different upbringing to my sisters—for which I am very grateful!

My parents made sure there was a lesson in everything, but there were two that really shaped me into who I am today:

1. the power of choice, and
2. living life with a positive mindset.

I never felt the urge to rebel, but I did challenge things that other people accepted as normal. The idea of just fitting in was never something I was interested in. I didn't want a normal life, and my parents showed me that I didn't have to.

By the time I was in high school, my parents had given me freedom, and, as long as I showed respect, I was free to do as I pleased. As a teenager, this was amazing but, coupled with going to one of Melbourne's top private all-boys schools, made me into somewhat of an arrogant smart-ass!

Looking back, I can pinpoint precisely when the smart-ass entrepreneurial spirit sparked within me. I was about fourteen, and I was being my usual smart-ass self. I made a comment to my father about my future being solid no matter what I did because of my "expected" inheritance. We were comfortable but by no means wealthy, and my inheritance had never been discussed. My father chuckled. "I've got news for you, my son. We don't plan on leaving anything to you!"

Snap! I was put straight back in my box. But the next day, my father handed me a book that changed my way of thinking forever: *Rich Dad Poor Dad* by Robert Kiyosaki. I won't recount the entire book but do yourself a favor and give it to your kids to read. Read it yourself if you haven't already.

The story follows Kiyosaki's upbringing and how he learned about money. He had what he describes as two dads. His "Poor Dad" was his biological father, an academic at a US University. Poor Dad always stressed the importance of getting an excellent education that would lead to a good job. Life sorted. His "Rich Dad" was his best friend's father, an entrepreneur and business owner who taught him that the only way to get ahead in life was to own your own business and that street smarts and learning about money, in the long run, would win over conventional education. For me, it all made sense.

Not only did this book flick a switch in my head, but I also saw a direct correlation between the two dads and my parents. My father had been in business for most of his adult life, starting his own pharmacy in a tiny forty-square-meter shop. He's the epitome of what I call "grinding it out." My father scraped up just enough money to put one of each product on the shelf and start the leanest pharmacy in history. When one product sold, he'd get enough money to put two back on the shelf, and his business grew from there. Over twenty years later, my father moved to a site five times the size and took over two shops on either side to have one of the biggest pharmacies in Melbourne at that time. He later sold the business and retired comfortably.

Having a Bachelor of Pharmacy (BPharm), he deemed education important but would always drive home the message that owning your own business was the only way to get ahead.

"But doctors make a lot of money; maybe I'll just become a doctor and own a surgery," I remember saying in my mid-teens.

"But GPs operate out of nothing more than a renovated house, so why would I want to buy your doctor's surgery when I can renovate the house next door and open up my own?" he refuted. He would constantly raise these valid points, and, subconsciously, I was learning.

My mother's view, on the other hand, was the opposite. She grew up in Murtoa, a small country town in Victoria, with only five other people graduating in her year at high school. As a result, education was deemed extremely important. If you didn't go to school and get a good education, you would either end up working at the wheat silos or on a farm for the rest of your life. University was your only chance to escape the town and move on to bigger and better things—or else you were stuck there! At least now I know where I got my passion for always demanding better for my life.

My mother went to university in Melbourne, became a home economics teacher, and had my eldest sister at twenty-two. After that, she had a career change and became the best mom in the world, who was also the best cook—with a degree to prove it! She was also Dad's biggest supporter in his business. Together, they made the perfect team. But to Mom, our future focus was always education and security: going to school, getting good grades, graduating university, and, finally, getting a good job. To me, that path led to joining the rat race, taking out a mortgage, living paycheck to paycheck, and fitting nicely into society. But that was way too normal for me—and normal just wouldn't cut it.

Kiyosaki's book changed the trajectory of my life. It was a pivotal point in my teenage years. I knew that I would own my own business one day, which led me to become a terrible employee—quite possibly the laziest one too.

MY INTRODUCTION TO THE SCHOOL OF HARD KNOCKS

My working career began at fifteen when I was earning $10 an hour in Dad's pharmacy. During this time, I had the opportunity to wear many hats. I was the mail

School of Hard Knocks.
Much of our education is to be obtained only in the school of hard knocks. There is no age limit and the sooner we are graduated the better for us.

boy (Australia Post representative), would empty the bins (waste disposal specialist), and then I'd hop on my bicycle and deliver prescriptions to sick customers in the local area (medicinal courier). A few years later, I was promoted to "shop assistant" or, as my brothers put it, "checkout chick." I was pretty good at dealing with customers, and I loved helping people. I also learned how to make people smile through compliments, joking around, and having fun. For me, it was the beginning of understanding the importance and power of human connection in business.

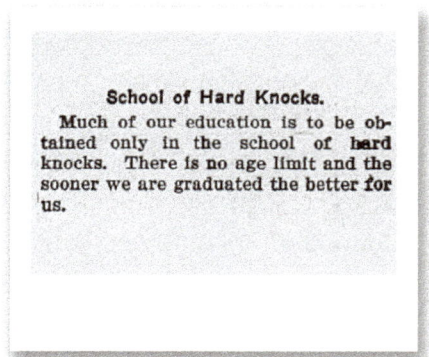

As an employee, I hated being told what to do. I found a reason to challenge everything. Being the boss's son gave me even more of a reason to rebel against authority. My constant cheekiness didn't go down well with the store managers, and my days at the pharmacy were numbered, even if my father was the owner.

Next, I tried the hospitality and gaming industry. Before discovering my love for health and fitness, I worked as a bartender and gaming cashier at a popular pokies venue in the Melbourne CBD: The Welcome Stranger. Falling under the Gaming code and award, the job paid more than a regular bar or nightclub gig, and the work was ten times easier. But that venue was the most depressing place of employment ever, and it certainly taught me what I didn't want to do. Customers were miserable and constantly complaining that they'd lost money. Then they would drown their sorrows in the aftermath.

One particular lady sticks out in my memory. She sat at the pokies for eight hours straight, dumping money into a $2 poker machine. I went up to her and asked her if she was okay and suggested that she take a break. Her reply, "I'm fine dear. My husband passed away not long ago, and he left me all of his money. I hated that son of a bitch, so the more of his money I lose, the happier I'll be!" Then there were the exciting moments when I would count out $20,000 in $50 notes to jackpot winners and celebrate with them and their newfound friends, knowing they'd gamble their winnings away the next day. Gambling addiction is very sad.

While there was never a dull moment working in the gaming industry, I was still lazy and never did more than expected. I was getting paid for my time, so in my mind, whether I worked hard or not, I would earn the same amount. I figured that the harder I worked, the more money the man at the top would make, which made the decision simple—I never worked hard. I had no passion and no drive to succeed. But I was good at saving, and with $20,000 in the bank, it was time to move on.

WHEN HEALTH AND FITNESS CHANGED MY LIFE

As a kid, I was always active and played many sports, but I was never health or fitness focused. I followed in the footsteps of my brothers and played basketball and AFL from an early age. At one stage, I was playing five games of basketball a week and considered myself reasonably good.

However, my body never reflected the effort I put in, as I had a compulsive eating problem from an early age. Food was comforting to me, and there was always junk in our pantry. The pantry was a waypoint to the main kitchen, and stopping there was like raiding the candy bar before heading in to see a movie. Sadly, I took advantage of this more than anyone else.

At seventeen, I was playing basketball and went for a simple lay-up, but I landed badly and dislocated my knee ninety degrees, snapping my anterior cruciate ligament (ACL), which is the main support ligament of the knee. I wouldn't be surprised if my weight were a significant factor in that injury. Apparently, on average, four times your body weight goes through your knees when you land from jumping. Two arthroscopies and a full knee reconstruction meant that my sporting career was sidelined for a whole year. Being inactive took its toll, and I got depressed. Food became my best friend. I remember the day I came out of surgery: it was the opening ceremony of the Sydney 2000 Olympics. Sitting in the same position in front of the TV for sixteen hours a day, I watched the Games— and I ate the whole time. When I finally got off the couch, my parents had to restuff it! I weighed 104 kilograms, and I felt like a blimp. I hated myself for abusing my body. I was meant to be in the prime of my life, but I was overweight and miserable.

I've had a compulsive eating problem for most of my life. After years of struggling, I can now say that I'm on top of it and can safely manage my compulsion. I've never found out why this happened, but an emotional switch would go off in my head, and I would just get the urge to eat junk. And it wasn't just a little bit of junk. I could down 5,000–7,000 calories easily in a thirty-minute sitting. I'd eat a box of barbecue shapes, a packet of Tim Tams, choc-chip cookies, any other biscuit I could get my hands on, and I would finish it off with ice cream and a Coke. During my binges, I *loved* it. All the chemicals, salt, and sugar made me feel amazing. But the aftermath was terrible. Not only would I feel sick, but I was gutted and ashamed that I had "done it again." Sometimes a binge would even result in me trying to throw up, which I never could. Looking back, I'm glad I could never throw anything up, as being able to do so may have led to something a lot worse.

I felt like my body was punishing me. I ate all that crap, so now I had to deal with what it would do to my body. They were dark times until, one day, I decided that I'd had enough. Here's a photo of me at seventeen years old when I was at my worst. But a lot has changed since then, and, unsurprisingly, no one knew who I was when I showed up at my ten-year school reunion!

It all changed in 2001 when I turned eighteen. Because I was still recovering from my knee reconstruction, I found myself starting to lift weights at lunchtime in the school gym, and it wasn't long until I realized I was naturally strong. I started entering bench press comps—no one knew who I was—and schoolyard arm wrestles. My strength gained

Year 12 high school photo, March 2001

Year 12 school formal and 18th birthday, June 2001

me respect among my peers, and, being solid growing up, I had quite a bit of muscle mass, which slowly began to show, under the fat. Then I tackled my diet. I began to eat cleaner, upping my protein intake and decreasing processed sugar, white bread, pasta, and starchy carbs. I became extremely disciplined and lost thirteen kilograms over four months. Week by week, my confidence grew. My passion for health and fitness had begun!

I finished year twelve with good grades, and, with no idea what I wanted to do, I found myself enrolled in a Bachelor of Science (BSc) at Monash University. By the middle of my first year at uni, I had gained seven kilograms of muscle, lost a further ten kilograms of fat, and was now weighing in at a ripped eighty-six kilograms. My confidence was through the roof. I started taking pride in my appearance, and girls began to notice me, which led to my first serious relationship.

At the gym six days a week, I surrounded myself with mates who also had a passion for weight training and would religiously study workout and diet plans online. I started buying bodybuilding and fitness magazines, spending all my money on supplements. I lived and breathed fitness. My life had changed entirely; I had re-invented who I was, and I loved it. I would study muscle anatomy, muscle attachments, and correct exercise execution and technique to trial in the gym. Different workouts fascinated me: pyramid training, strength training, hypertrophy versus endurance, high-intensity interval training—the list goes on. I loved it all and found that I was the happiest I had been my entire life.

Arnold Schwarzenegger sums it up better than I can in what is by far my favorite quote:

"When your vision is powerful enough, everything else falls into place: how you live your life, your workouts, what friends you choose to hang out with, how you eat, what you do for fun. Vision is purpose, and when your purpose is clear so are your life choices. Vision creates faith and faith creates willpower. With faith there is no anxiety, no doubt—just absolute confidence." [1]

WHEN BUSINESS CALLS, BUT NO ONE IS HOME

In 2003, I was in my second year of uni, and I still had no clue what I wanted to do. I attempted subjects like finance, marketing, and accounting, thinking I needed to know something about each if I were to start my own business—but I failed all of them. Halfway through my second year, to my mother's absolute dismay, I deferred my studies and started my own distributor business with a health and wellness multi-level marketing company, selling nutritional products. *This was it. This was my chance*—or so I thought. Ha! I lost my $20,000 life savings in six months and hated every minute of it. I knew nothing about business, and I knew nothing about selling let alone selling products that I didn't even believe in. I quit.

My father saw this as a learning curve for me, and my mother saw it as the perfect opportunity to stress how important education was, so I went back to doing what I loved: exercise and fitness. I completed my Certificate III and IV in Fitness and Personal Training, went back to uni, and changed my subjects to double major in what interested me the most: the body (physiology) and what you could put in to change it (pharmacology).

In 2004, after obtaining my personal training certifications and while finishing my second year at university, I worked at King Club Health and Fitness, an institution in the south-eastern suburbs of Melbourne. I'll never forget my first three weeks there, which set me up for my career in the fitness industry. My manager at the time, Pam, informed me that all she wanted me to do in my first twelve shifts was talk to members. That's it. I wasn't allowed to train them or even do assessments. That was five to seven hours per shift, for twelve shifts in total, of just talk. At first, I hated it—and Pam for that matter! I would constantly hide in the toilets and was completely out of my comfort zone, randomly walking up to people to say hello and introducing myself as the new recruit on the block. But it was those three weeks that changed the way I communicated with people. I learned a precious lesson that would set me up in this industry—and life. By asking the right questions, engaging people personally, and making them feel comfortable, they would warm to me and be open to working with me. I was never selling them anything, just myself as an individual. To this day, I thank Pam for her brutal introduction to the fitness industry. It changed a lot for me.

As the job went on, I connected more and more with clients. I'd been on my own weight loss journey, and I understood what it felt like to be uncomfortable in your skin and all the emotions associated with wanting to lose weight. I would ask clients to stand in front of the mirror in their underwear for up to five minutes. They needed to see what they disliked. It was a powerful motivator for change. I wanted to train everyone—body-builders, moms and dads, fitness newbies, seniors—you name it. I wanted to connect and help people get leaner and stronger. Over two years, I focused on getting to know and connect with as many people as I could. It wasn't long before I gained a reputation as a specialist in strength and conditioning and getting people from all walks of life great results.

While I was a great trainer and good with clients, I was *still* a terrible employee. I maintained the mentality that I could always do things better and that I wasn't just going to work in a gym my whole life for $22 an hour. I asked myself: for whom was I working so hard? An obese gym owner and his overweight daughter/manager, neither of whom I'd ever seen exercise in the gym? So, I started taking the piss. During my Sunday shifts on the gym floor, I'd duck away for free solariums (stupid, I know, but it was all the rage back then). I would also take unauthorized "lunch breaks" during which I'd get in fifty laps in the pool or do a workout while on duty with a mate. It wasn't long before I was in the manager's office being asked to commit to the job or leave. Two months later, I left.

I wanted more for my life, and I wanted more from the Australian fitness industry. I tried to find something completely different from what was then being offered in Australia. The personal training industry was already saturated, and I knew that wasn't where I wanted to be forever. The only way to make money was to work more hours, so I would never see my personal trainer friends because they were always working. Even to this day, I cringe when people tell me they're opening a personal training gym, as I know they've bought themselves a tireless job. That's just not part of my business mentality. I realized that I wasn't going to find what I was looking for on Australian shores. So, in the summer of that year, I quit the King Club and bought a ticket to the US searching for something…

LAND OF THE ENTREPRENEUR

I fell in love with the US instantly. Things were bigger, and the people were loud, fun, and crazy. These were my kind of people! Opportunity was everywhere, and entrepreneurialism was encouraged. Have an idea? Then go out and make it happen. That's the American dream, and everyone has the right to it. And if you fail, that's okay! You had a crack, and they'll support you to try again.

Being an avid snowboarder, it wasn't long until I was in the Vail Valley in Colorado, home to some of the best ski terrain in the world. I got a job as a personal trainer and snowshoe instructor at the Park Hyatt gym in the illustrious Beaver Creek Mountain Resort. It was common knowledge that if you were rich and famous and wanted to be seen, you would go to Aspen in Colorado, but if you had real wealth and didn't want to be seen, you went to Beaver Creek. This is where I learned the difference between the rich and the wealthy. The truth? The rich work for the wealthy.

The roads on the mountain were heated, and the trees lit up with fairy lights at night. Ski valets were employed solely to put guests' skis on and take them off at the end of a session to store for the next day's skiing.

Oh, and the ladies and their fur! Brands like Moncler, Canada Goose, and Louis Vuitton were household names. It was in this job that I learned to deal with the incredibly wealthy. With my Aussie accent and charm, coupled with my experience at the King Club, I became a world-class schmoozer. Huge New York business tycoons would often holiday with their family, coming in via private jet. I would train the husband in the gym before he took the kids skiing for the day, and then I'd take the wife on a snowshoe tour before she'd shack up in the day spa for the remaining hours of the day. I even wore an excellent fake Bvlgari watch that received compliments daily. Fake it until you make it! I was in their world now, so I had to act like it.

Best of all, private clients meant money. American labor rates were—and still are—horrific. Gym floor staff earned US$8 an hour, and the front counter staff made US$12. And, unlike most service-industry jobs in the US, they never got tips. Yet, I would take a client on a walk in the snow for ninety minutes and earn US$100, including a $20–$50 tip! You can guess what I got good at. I soon became the most popular snowshoe instructor on the mountain, working just sixteen hours a week on average for that entire season. I would earn more in a week than a gym instructor earned working full-time in a month. This enabled me to snowboard almost every day, and I had to take Thursdays off just to give my body a rest.

LOST ON THE MOUNTAIN

One day while snowboarding, I found myself in real strife. I was up on the hill, and, as it hadn't snowed for a few days, I went off-piste to chase some fresh powder. I accidentally went over one valley too far and found some of the best and deepest snow I had ever ridden. It was amazing, but I was too busy having fun to notice that I was going completely the wrong way. I ended up at the bottom of a gully in the middle of nowhere. Knowing I would have to hike out, I unstrapped my board, stepped out, and immediately sunk over my waist in fresh snow. Shit. I was in deep trouble. After half an hour of commando crawling through the snow, I had only moved about thirty meters, and I was exhausted due to the altitude. It was also about 2 pm, so I knew I only had limited daylight hours left, as the sun would set at 4:30 pm. With no phone on me (idiot), I was convinced I would be spending the night out, which scared the absolute hell out of me. The silence was also a reminder of just how alone I was.

The sun was going down, and the night's cold was setting in. I'm not talking Australian Alps -5°C cold, but -30°C cold. Three hours passed, and I was stuffed: tired, hungry, thirsty, and cold. Then I caught a glimpse of a small orange ribbon tied to a branch. Just ahead, I saw another one. Thinking back to my scouting days, I was praying that it was an orienteering course that led back to the resort runs, so I crawled up the hill enough to strap my board back on and get some speed. Slowly, I used trees to push me in the direction of each ribbon, all of my focus on the next flash of orange. After about twenty minutes, I found myself at the bottom of a resort run on the furthest side of the mountain. I'd found my way back. I was so relieved! The lift had closed for the day, but I saw an attendant in the cabin signing off on the day's work—he was shocked to see me. I told him what had happened, and he explained how lucky I was, that I'd ended up in a national forest outside of the ski patrol boundary, and how the situation could have ended a lot worse. He fired up the lift; we both jumped on, and he took me back to the safety of the resort village. Getting lost in the snow shook me to the core and made me realize how precious life is.

GETTING MY DEGREE

At the beginning of 2005, my working holiday visa came to an end, and the final year of my degree called me home—very much in the voice of my mother. I found myself back in Melbourne to finish my Bachelor of Science (BSc) with a double major in exercise physiology and pharmacology. I didn't want to work in gyms again, so I got a job as a research assistant and personal trainer at Deakin University in the health and nutrition faculty. I found the research interesting, but, after doing non-stop experiments all day, it wasn't long before I realized that this career path again was not for me.

I still remember my associate professor sitting me down and asking what I really wanted to do with my life and career. I still had no idea, but I knew that research wasn't it. But he still tried to pump it up, telling me to seriously consider research as a career path. "I earn over $100,000 a year. I drive a nice company car. Hell, I don't even do much work anymore. It's a comfortable life." And that was great for him, but I didn't want to be comfortable. I found out that he was fired two years later, so it looks like he became a little too relaxed!

Although Deakin University didn't provide the right answers for me, it did provide me with a much more rewarding outcome, as it enabled me to work and save. I now had the travel bug. For six months, I did nothing but work, save, and train. The opportunity to travel again came up, so I took off around the world. I was on the search. For what exactly, I didn't know at the time, just something more, something better, something different. Unsatisfied with my life in Melbourne, I set a date for the beginning of a three-year overseas adventure.

LESSONS LEARNED

1. Never assume you have it made because you grew up comfortable. Always look for opportunities to make your own way. The faster you get out of your comfort zone, the faster you will find out who YOU really are.

2. Life is about choice. The faster you realize this, the quicker you can do or have anything you want. YOU are in the pilot's seat, so your imagination is the only thing that limits the direction you go.

3. If you have no drive and no passion for what you do, it's time you started looking for something else. Working in a job you hate for forty years doesn't show commitment; it shows that you didn't have enough courage to make a change and move on. Not making a decision *is* making a decision.

"Travel often;
getting lost will help
you find yourself."

—Holstee Manifesto

Chapter 2

TRAVEL—MY MOST IMPORTANT TEACHER

Travel for me meant freedom. In March 2006, the most exciting place in the world for me was on the other side of the departure gates at Melbourne International Airport. While others were getting teary with their families and loved ones in front of the sliding doors, I couldn't wait to walk through them. Those doors were the gateway to adventure and excitement where there were no rules, no boundaries. I could do whatever and go wherever I wanted. I was free.

I was lucky enough to share the beginning of my adventure with one of my best mates, Rick. We met in our first year of high school when we were

It was at this threshold that I understood the real value of choice. In our day-to-day lives, it's so easy to conform to society's norms and put ourselves in a box with the rest of the boring world and, worst of all, get stuck in the rat race. It's only when you realize the box is fictional and you can challenge the rules that you see the world differently. All of a sudden, your eyes open.

about twelve years old. I thought I was one of the most easy-going people around until I met Rick. Our adventures were wild, and our experiences were priceless: from cage diving with great white sharks in South Africa, running with the bulls in Spain, being held at gunpoint in the Caribbean by local militia, to watching the Aussies win the 2007 Cricket World Cup in Barbados. We participated in spring break in Mexico, Oktoberfest in Germany, and had sleepless nights in Vegas and Hong Kong (China). I had so much fun, met so many people, and had some of the best experiences of my life. I could write a whole other book on my shoestring travel adventures spanning three years and thirty-eight countries, but, when it comes to life and learning, one adventure stands out.

We were on the island of Grenada in the Caribbean and had a few days between cricket matches. Instead of staying in the capital of St George's to party with the rest of the World Cup cricket fanatics, we decided to hire a car and go on a beach camping adventure to explore the island. Sleeping arrangements were already sorted, as we each had a blowup air mattress that we'd been using to relax in the ocean on beach days. We also had a couple of Heineken promotional tarps that we'd "found" at a local gathering one night, and we could use them to cover us if it rained. We drove north, and, at some stage, we decided to do a bit of off-roading to find a beach to set up our makeshift camp. For two hours, we drove on dirt and sand tracks until the road came to an end. By this stage, it was

Table Mountain, Cape Town South Africa, 2008

Coco Hotel, Dominican Republic, 2007 (with Rick Caldow)

Big White Mountain, Canada, January 2009

dark, and we had no idea where we were. After grabbing our stuff and leaving the car, we trekked in sand dunes for a few hundred meters until the terrain flattened, and we knew we had hit a beach. The moon was shining off the water, silence was in the air, and there wasn't a person or any sign of civilization in sight. Or so we thought.

By the time we settled down with a couple of beers by the fire, it would have been after midnight. I noticed movement in the distance, a few silhouettes walking along the water's edge. This seemed a bit strange, as we were literally in the middle of nowhere, not a light in sight. Although we couldn't see them, we knew that with the fire blazing, they could see us. A thousand scenarios of this whole adventure going horribly wrong played out in our heads. Then we lost the shadowy figures in the darkness and began to shit ourselves even more.

Fifteen minutes later, we heard a voice, and we both jumped up as a man appeared. He politely asked us to put out our fire. It turned out that the beach we had found was the nesting grounds for the giant leatherback turtle, the largest species of all living turtles. The man headed up a research group that monitored and studied these unique and endangered species, which can grow to two meters long and more than one meter high. When the turtles come up onto the beach to lay their eggs, they do so in a trance-like state but are attracted to bright lights, such as our fire. Any turtles that saw the flames would end up laying their eggs too far up the beach for their young to get back to sea once hatched.

He asked us if we wanted to see what he was talking about, so we put the fire out and walked down to the water's edge to see a giant leatherback turtle come in from the sea. Slow and steady, we followed this fantastic creature up the beach until she found the right place to stop. Half an hour later, after digging her nest in the sand, we were in awe as thirty-seven eggs came out of the mother, with a research volunteer catching and counting them in the process. A few minutes later, she filled in the hole and returned to the sea. Thinking that this was a random occurrence, Rick and I high fived each other and were soon on our way when the professor noted that this would be happening all night. We spent the next two hours watching countless giant turtles come up and lay their eggs.

I believe that everything happens for a reason. That whole experience taught me that only when you do something different, when you're bold enough to leave your comfort zone and go beyond what everyone else is doing, will you find something special. I would have chosen that time on the beach over drinking in countless bars back in the main town any day of the week. It was one of the most incredible experiences of my entire life.

LONDON CALLING

After the first twelve months of travel, my money ran out. I wasn't ready to come home, so I set myself up in London. I had met a South African girl who made my decision to base myself there a little easier, and my new London life began. Although I'd previously worked as a personal trainer, I didn't want to go back to working in a gym. However, I did teach a few clients in Hyde Park, mainly for the experience of getting out and about.

I picked up some work as a laborer from my flatmates in the building industry. Throughout the day, I would cart buckets and buckets of cement from the mixer to the pour site time and time again. It was the most boring thing I've ever done in my life. If you think you'd get fit from all the manual labor, think again. When you do something so boring, you tend to drink at night to forget how much your life sucks. We'd also have 6–8 smokos (snack breaks) during the day just to have something to look forward to, so the weight slowly crept on. I knew this was not healthy, so it wasn't long until I gave that job the flick, and the search continued. Plus, the seven pounds an hour just wasn't cutting it.

As well as searching for work, I began checking out the London fitness scene in more depth. Big gym chains like Fitness First and Virgin Active were popular, but I noticed that small boutique group fitness was rising. The main difference was that they focused on a more personalized approach.

One day I came across an ad for a "Dynamic Pilates Instructor" at a boutique studio called Beautcamp—now Bootcamp—Pilates in London's prestigious West End. Intrigued, I applied. The next day I was called in for an interview and booked into a class. I was familiar with Pilates, but, in the Australian market, it was being bolted on to every physio clinic as rehab Pilates. The physiotherapy world had adopted a brilliant idea, doubling the longevity of a client by moving them to the Pilates side of the business once physio treatment was complete.

But this Pilates studio was different, and the method of training wasn't what I expected. I immediately fell in love with the high-performance element of the method. The style originated in Los Angeles, and the owner of Bootcamp used to be a client of the US founder, Sebastien Lagree, who eventually went on to reinvent his own style of fitness: the Lagree Method. Bootcamp was the first studio of its kind in London, so it was exciting to be a part of something fresh, new, and different.

The studio was small and incredibly hard to find—but extremely popular. Bootcamp Pilates didn't need to be on the main street. It was a destination, and the fact that it was difficult to find made it more exclusive and desirable. The head trainer was also an Aussie, which helped me get the job, and we got along straight away. For the next six weeks, I was in that studio 30+ hours per week, training and getting trained in the method of dynamic Pilates, integrating with trainers, getting to know the clients, and loving every minute. I also saw excellent results. My travels and failed laboring career had added extra bodyweight, which I quickly stripped off with Pilates and was looking quite fit again. As I trained, I worked muscles I didn't even know existed, and I felt incredible. The crucial thing was that the trainer didn't do the class with the group. Instead, he or she would run around and put clients in the correct positions, adding that personal element as much as possible. I had found something that I wanted to learn absolutely everything about.

One exciting part of training at the studio was how the London Pilates world perceived us. In the city's traditional and proper Pilates circles, we were frowned upon and seen as rebels, which suited my personality to a tee. Our style replaced the perfect form and technique known to traditionalists with a fast-paced, full-body workout that worked clients to the point of fatigue. Posh elderly London teachers were replaced with younger international trainers, most of whom were strapping young males who pumped the music up every chance they'd get. Classes were also performed on a spring resistance Pilates reformer machine, getting people up off the floor and away from traditional mat work. This allowed people to experience the equipment's capabilities from a beginner level. In contrast, in most other Pilates studios at the time, you had to be intermediate or advanced before you were given the green light to use any additional Pilates apparatus.

The buzz and excitement around such a small studio were incredible, and the media loved us too. We were frequently featured as London's number one fitness craze in all of the glossy magazines. The buzz also brought actors, models, and all sorts of UK and international celebrities in, which helped with our positioning in the marketplace. That was the turning point for me. Within those first few weeks, I knew that *this* was what I was going to bring back to Australia. But first, I had to perfect my teaching and build a reputation and following in London.

Customer service and personal touch were essential at Bootcamp Pilates. In the beginning, with only six clients per class, I excelled at giving an exceptional experience and workout. I learned everything there was to learn about the client: their name, profession, family, hobbies, pets, and holiday destinations. I was a sponge before, during, and after every class. Afterward, I would write down all the information I'd gathered and study it. Before my next shift, I would look ahead and see who was attending my classes, go back to my notes, and refresh my memory.

When you're a trainer, physical touch is essential to make sure clients are doing exercises correctly. It's vital to make them feel safe and unique. I was always kind and respectful, never crossing the line into social relationships, although I was constantly invited to dinners and drinks. I turned those clients down each time and, instead, trained them extra hard the next day when they came in hungover.

PROFESSIONAL BOUNDARIES

When I first studied personal training at nineteen, my teacher was a success-ful fitness franchisor who explained the reality of the industry and that most of our clients are female. "In this industry, all you have is your reputation. You can attract huge success, a big following, and you'll be put in situations where clients will want to date you. Sleeping with your clients isn't difficult. It *is* difficult to not cross boundaries and remain professional at all times. All you need is one slipup to ruin everything, and your reputation is gone." So, right then and there, I decided that I would never cross that line. To this day, I'm proud to say that I have always maintained my professionalism.

It wasn't long until the first Bootcamp studio was booked solid, and classes had substantial waiting lists. Therefore, we had to move to bigger premises and make more noise in the fitness scene. With the move came more space and access to additional foot traffic, as the new studio was on a main street. I also learned how easy it was to move an established business. Because we had built such fantastic rapport with our clients, I would say that ninety-nine percent followed us to the new location. We went from teaching six people to ten in each class, increasing revenue overnight by over sixty percent. And so, the next chapter of Bootcamp Pilates began.

The lack of leadership at the top of Bootcamp Pilates suited my per-sonality. The owner was an investor, and the business didn't use the owner/operator model that you see in KX studios. You would never see the owner nor hear from her. She never managed or led the team at all. Looking back, she was lucky that she had trainers who were self-motivated and self-managed. When I worked there, I treated it like my own studio, and I was my own boss, creating my own personal brand under her banner. I felt like these were *my* clients. I immediately knew that this studio was different from any other I had been in, and, although poorly run, Bootcamp Pilates signified where the fitness industry was headed; the rise of boutique fitness had begun. I would often visualize that it was my studio and that I was back in Australia.

The nature of a boutique fitness studio worked thanks to its customized approach through:

1. Personalization

2. Systemization

3. Accountability

1. Personalization

As a trainer, I made it my mission to know everyone's name. I used the five-minute warm-up to connect with clients, look them in the eye, and make them feel welcome. At night, I would study neuro-linguistic programming (NLP), learning the difference between audio, visual, and kinesthetic people, and I changed my teaching style to reflect each client's response. Some clients liked a more dominating training approach; others preferred a more timid and quiet push. Being able to adapt to each client was vital. I would bring my bubbly personality out throughout the class, constantly adjusting and putting people in the correct position. Ten minutes post-class was left for questions, demonstrating and assisting different stretches, or more time to connect.

2. Systemization

Everything was done online. We had our own customized booking software linked to the website that allowed clients to book, pay, and cancel online. Trainers didn't have to handle payments or cash often, which reduced the need for a full-time receptionist. The studio was so simple to run, and apps weren't even around back then. Everything was still done via desktop, and it worked.

3. Accountability

Bootcamp had no lock-in contracts, no membership fees, and no joining fees from the business side. Instead, packs of one, five, ten, or twenty sessions were available and valid anywhere between three and six months. "Pay for when you come, not for when you don't" was the pricing slogan. That meant that if you didn't shine in the client's eyes, they might not come back to your class or the studio at all. We were constantly kept on our toes and couldn't afford to have an off day.

Accountability lay with the client and came in the form of the booking and cancellation policy. We were brutal with our twelve-hour cancellation policy. Any class canceled within that timeframe would be deducted, so clients had a pretty good reason not to skip or cancel a class once they had booked.

In the two years I taught at Bootcamp Pilates' West End studio, I saw massive growth in our style of fitness. Trainers and clients often approached the owner of Bootcamp to open more studios in additional boroughs across London, but she would always pass on those offers. Although she had her own growth plans, bringing on partners at that time was something she opposed. One by one, I witnessed the initial four trainers who'd started with me leave and open their own dynamic Pilates studios under their own brands. In two years, I saw the dynamic Pilates concept grow from one studio to fifteen across five different brands in London, solidifying my vision to take it back to Australia.

DOROTHY WAS RIGHT: THERE'S NO PLACE LIKE HOME

Often, when young Australians end up in London, their friends start to ask, "What will you do when you return home?" For two years, I told everyone that I would start my own dynamic Pilates studio in Australia when I was ready to return. Although, this affirmation proved difficult to say around my then girlfriend. We had been seeing each other for a while and had moved in together. She had no intention of leaving London because she had a great job, amazing friends, and some of her family by her side. But for me, it was inevitable that the ride would soon be over.

To this day, I still remember when everything changed. On a sunny day in April 2009, I was walking through Hyde Park after training some clients. It was a beautiful day—about 18°C, which was hot for UK standards—and because the sun was out, so was everyone in London, trying to tan their winter-white bodies. The weather had been amazing for three weeks. Because of a freezing and miserable winter, people were excited for summer, which was just around the corner. It was at that moment, walking through the park and observing the changing of seasons, that I knew I was done. Change was in the air, and it was also inside me. I felt like London was not the place for me anymore. It was time to go home, spend lost time with my family and old friends, chase my dreams, and leave my London life behind. The thought was thrilling yet upsetting, as I had built a great life there. My relationship was amazing, and I often traveled. I also had wonderful friends and solid employment where I earned good money. But all of those things just weren't enough. It was time to go home.

In my mind, the decision was final, and, that night, I went home and told my girlfriend that I had decided to return to Australia in the coming months. Surprisingly, she completely understood. I'm pretty sure there was a part of her that had expected it. I had been talking about taking the dynamic style of Pilates home for a long time, and she saw the passion I had in my eyes. She knew that she couldn't stand in the way of my dreams. She also realized that she might not be in them. We both agreed then and there that we'd enjoy every last moment we had together in the eight weeks before I left the UK. A few days later, we had booked multiple weekend trips to Switzerland, France, and Italy. Lastly, I booked my ticket home to Australia.

My final two months in the UK were probably my favorite. We had the most amazing time in some of the most spectacular cities in the world, and I'll never forget them. But, once again, I had direction and a clear vision, which renewed my enthusiasm. I felt alive because I was back on the chase. I had already started planning the business and thinking of names. Soon, the KX Pilates name was born. At that point, the K and X didn't stand for anything; I pronounced it "kicks," which I thought was fitting due to the amount of legwork in the workout.

To say the day of my departure was emotional would be an under-statement. We spent most of the day playing tourists in London, ticking off the sights that I was yet to see and just enjoying life. As she tried to stay strong, my girlfriend handed me a parting gift. When I unwrapped it, tears ran down my face. It was a wooden plaque with the words "KX Pilates" carved into it. "Go and chase your dreams," she said. "I would say good luck, but luck has nothing to do with it, as you will be the one who will make KX Pilates amazing."

That chapter of my life may have come to a close, but I'll always cherish the fond memories we had together and hold a certain appreciation for her being one of the first people to believe in my vision. Still, to this day, the KX Pilates plaque she gave me is on the front door of my very first studio in Malvern, Victoria.

Studio #1 - KX Pilates Malvern (VIC)

LESSONS LEARNED

1. Travel—only when you get out of your comfort zone and experience what the world has to offer do you see the world differently. Your eyes will open, and you'll see opportunities you've never seen before.

2. Chase your dreams, no matter how big they might seem, and be prepared to give everything up to go after them. I would rather have failed but known that I tried than never to have tried at all.

3. Be curious and question everything. Learn from people's great ideas *and* their mistakes. I saw why Bootcamp Pilates succeeded and saw how it had squandered its full potential by staying small and not being open to opportunity.

"Change happens
through movement,
and movement heals."

—Joseph Pilates

Chapter 3

WHAT EXACTLY IS PILATES?

You may be asking yourself: what even is Pilates? And you wouldn't be the first, nor will you be the last. At its core, Pilates is a form of low-impact exercise that takes place on a mat or specialized pieces of equipment, the most commonly known being a reformer. Generally, the practice emphasizes the mind-body connection, and focuses on improving strength, flexibility, and balance. While Pilates isn't traditionally a cardio workout, more intense flavors—like what we do at KX—will leave you sweating as your muscles beg for mercy.

Precision, control, and technique are all important. While a certain amount of physical effort is required, no one should overlook the mental aspects of the practice. As with any type of exercise, good form is critical.

Exercises include planks, leg lifts, hip dips, scissor kicks, and more. With added equipment, such as circles, poles, and the infamous reformer, a Pilates workout is super effective, endlessly versatile, and always exciting.

Because Pilates is low-impact, the practice is ideal for almost any age group, fitness level, or ability. Beginners can dive in with enthusiasm, while more advanced students can always find new ways to challenge themselves. Pilates really is one of the most inclusive forms of fitness out there, and, when you learn where it came from, you'll understand why.[2]

JOSEPH PILATES, THE FATHER OF PILATES

Whatever Pilates is now, the practice wouldn't exist without its founder, Joseph Pilates. Originally a boxer and circus performer, the German-born fitness enthusiast developed his new workout style while interned in an English World War I internment camp. No one can say that he didn't make the most of his downtime.

Due to a lack of resources in the camp, Joseph was forced to think creatively and make resistance equipment out of whatever items were convenient at the time—anything he could get his hands on. Some rumors suggest that the inspiration for the Pilates Circle came from using the metal rings from the beer kegs of that era. Joseph's seemingly endless supply of creativity soon led to the invention of the reformer machine. While his initial model looks a lot different from the KXformer we use in our studios today, the basic concepts are there. The man wasn't just an innovator but a legitimate inventor as well.

With his newly developed exercise regime, Joseph helped train and rehabilitate other prisoners, many suffering from sickness or injury. While he may not have been pushing his patients to do the intense, muscle-burning workouts we enjoy at KX, his actions had a clear purpose. From the beginning, Pilates was a tool for change, development, and growth.

When the war ended, Joseph taught Pilates in Germany before going to New York to train students and develop the first generation of teachers, known as the Elders. His new disciples would share their knowledge and help spread the practice across the country. While some former students taught Joseph's methods precisely, others adapted their own styles. Pilates is a practice that has never stopped evolving.

In 1967, at eighty-three years old, Joseph Pilates passed away. By all accounts, he never lost his fitness nor his enthusiasm for the innovative style of exercise he'd created. It's a shame he wasn't around to see his humble creation become the popular, widespread, and beloved practice it is today.[3]

Joe Pilates, Inventor, physical fitness guru and founder of the Pilates exercise method demonstrates his techniques in his 8th Avenue studio on October 4, 1961 in New York City, New York.

UNDENIABLE BENEFITS OF PILATES

While some of the benefits of Pilates—improved fitness, increased strength, better health—may be obvious, not all the perks of the practice are immediately apparent. Anyone who spends time in a studio or embarks on their Pilates journey via some other route soon understands the positive impact the exercises can have. For me, Pilates was love at first sight—or first sweat—for a reason.

1. Enhance Mind-Body Connection

While Pilates doesn't focus on the spiritual, it's also not a purely physical practice. The precision and balance required to perform some exercises can't help but enhance your mind-body connection. When you start training in Pilates, you must learn to listen to your body in order to reach peak proficiency. Proper breathing and a flawless form are more important than raw power. Although, at KX, a little energy and enthusiasm is encouraged.

2. Increase Flexibility

Flexibility may not be the primary goal of a Pilates practitioner, but it is a noteworthy side effect of the workouts we do. Many movements don't just train strength but joint mobility and flexibility as well. With Pilates, you lengthen and strengthen at the same time. What a great deal!

3. Strengthen and Condition the Entire Body

Because Pilates is a full body workout, you avoid creating muscle imbalances, which can lead to injury and general discomfort. Your body is a single, complex unit, and everything is connected. Pilates recognizes this and provides a balanced workout that targets every muscle, including those in the feet, ankles, and hands, to sculpt you into a well-conditioned machine. When you practice Pilates, staying strong and avoiding injury is easy.

Being fit and healthy alone is enough to generate a whole load of benefits for your body and mind, and Pilates allows you to develop tough physical and mental attributes in a safe, fun, and effective way. While Pilates has grown in popularity over the past few decades, it's not something that everyone practices or is even aware of. When you walk into a studio pumped and ready for a session, it feels like you're entering an exclusive club. You know you're about to get an amazing workout with an enthusiastic group of people, and only a select few are in on the secret. But Pilates isn't an exclusive movement—it's a club that anyone can join—and whoever discovers this dynamic form of fitness can experience big improvement in their overall health and wellbeing. For a lot of us, Pilates really is a game changer.[4]

PILATES TRADEMARK CONTROVERSY AND LAWSUIT

Until October 2000, the law forbade instructors and studios from using the word Pilates. Sean Gallagher, a studio owner in Manhattan, had trademarked the term and refused to share it with others. He argued that only he and his instructors were teaching a legitimate form of the practice; therefore, he deserved sole ownership of the name. His statement was far from true, as the court found that numerous qualified instructors were operating in the US.

After Gallagher filed a lawsuit against Current Concepts (now

Balanced Body) and company founder, Ken Endelman, for using the Pilates name, in an act of good sense, Manhattan's federal court invalidated the trademark, stating that Pilates is a generic term used to describe a specific form of exercise—a win for instructors and studios everywhere. I can only imagine the creative ways that people would say Pilates without actually saying the word. Did they mime it? Use code words? Write "not-Pilates" on their studio signage? Thankfully, it's one issue KX never had to deal with.[5]

WHAT IS THE KX METHOD AND HOW DOES IT DIFFER FROM TRADITIONAL PILATES?

KX Pilates is a combination of traditional Pilates and the strengthening and toning aspects of circuit training. Our dynamic, fast-paced, high-performance, full-body workouts are fifty minutes long, with a maximum of fourteen people per class. Exercises are performed on a customized spring resistance apparatus called a KXformer machine, specifically designed for KX and our style of training. Most generic reformers include 3–6 springs of varying tensions—often color coded—that you can easily clip on and off.

When using a reformer, resistance comes from multiple spring loads. A carriage, which moves up and down a set of rails, is linked to these springs, and movement can occur by either pushing away with your feet on the foot bar or pulling the hand/foot straps connected via ropes and pulleys. Unlike lifting weights and competing with the resistance of gravity, the reformer allows for smooth movement where spring resistance and body weight are the load. As the carriage moves further, the spring tension increases, and additional resistance is automatically applied.

Movements can either focus on increasing resistance or controlling the decreased resistance of the spring load. While some exercises, such as a chest press or plank, may seem quite simple, the spring tension of the reformer adds a layer of difficulty you won't get from a closed-loop chest press machine at the gym or by planking on the floor. On top of that, the increased focus on core stability during each exercise provides additional challenge and benefits.

The beauty of the KXformer is that it allows us to work all areas of the body while improving not just strength and endurance, but balance, coordination, and flexibility as well. Exercises can be compound, using multiple muscle groups, or isolation, focusing on just one muscle group. Our training techniques utilize the isolate-fatigue-stretch principle, which means exactly what it suggests. We isolate the muscle group(s), fatigue them, and stretch them. During a session, the KX Trainer will decide whether or not to focus on a specific muscle group, but, either way, you'll always receive a full body workout.

Unlike some other group reformer classes, we aim to sequence exercises in a way that ensures minimal spring and prop changes for maximum intensity. At KX, other apparatuses include jump boards, sitting boxes, Pilates rings, dumbbells, bungee resistance straps, and weighted poles and balls. Depending on the exercise, we can use props to either increase or decrease difficulty or simply help with balance. In the case of the jump board, the reformer turns into a plyometric cardio jumping machine. At KX, we also superset—move right from one exercise into another— between the upper and lower body, which allows us to rest the muscles we've just been working without decreasing heart rate or intensity.

Using the KX "eight points of teaching" training principles, we also teach our Trainers how to freestyle their classes, while constantly main- taining KX Pilates methodology. Meaning you could come to KX seven days a week, and each workout would be different. It's up to our Trainers to create session plans, add their own personality and flair, and make each class their own. This level of personalization is what our clients come back for. Unlike a spin class, where you know what you're getting every time, KX keeps you guessing. Even something as simple as teaching a class in reverse order completely throws the sequence on its head, as the muscle fatigue reversed makes certain exercises challenging in new ways.

For your very first class, we'll give you a tour of the studio. You'll also receive a lot more attention before and after the session. For example, we'll introduce you to the KXformer and show you step-by-step how to use the machine and associated props. We'll also discuss any injuries or limitations you might have and provide alternatives to exercises you can't fully perform during the workout. It's important to note that KX is NOT rehab Pilates. While we can work with little niggling injuries, a serious injury could mean that KX classes aren't for you until you've recovered.

Importantly, Trainers will instruct both regressions—for those not as strong, fit, or have limitations due to injury—and progressions to exercises, for those who want to challenge themselves even more. This approach allows clients to make each class their own. Although everyone performs the same workout at the same time, slight changes to exercises allow us to tailor the class to the individual. Due to this, clients at different levels can participate in the same beginner or intermediate sessions. However, I would never recommend that a beginner go to an advanced class, as the competency requirements greatly increase.

All classes start the same, with clients lying on their backs, feet to the ceiling, using the Pilates ring and stretching their hamstrings. Starting like this allows for a smooth transition into the warm-up. However, clients are welcome to use the ten-minute gap between classes to stretch or prepare for the class in their own way.

Warm-ups are a 5–7-minute sequence of light exercises that target the entire body. Each Trainer has a slightly different way of doing things—we encourage individuality! Once you're warmed up, the bulk of the class plan begins. Each exercise sequence is timed, meaning we don't count reps, and you're able to move at the pace your body and fitness allow. You're also in your own "zone," so the only person you're competing with is yourself. At any time, you can stop or slow down an exercise, get a drink, towel off, or simply catch your breath if needed. You perform the workout all to the beat of your own drum.

KX workouts—as opposed to traditional reformer Pilates—include many compound exercises, such as squats, lunges, chest presses, and more. Firing multiple muscles at once elevates heart rate and keeps classes intense. Exercises are performed at medium load, usually for 1–3 minutes each, to enable a high volume of repetitions. For maximum efficiency, sequences can last anywhere from 3–10 minutes.

At KX, our Trainers don't participate in the classes when they're teaching. Instead, they explain each exercise comprehensively and may use a client to showcase a movement. If a spare machine is available, Trainers may choose to demonstrate an exercise themselves. By keeping themselves free, they can instruct the class more easily and approach each client to offer specific feedback and personalized attention before moving on.

Music is important at KX, but classes aren't choreographed or performed to a specific beat. Instead, we use music as a tool to bring energy and excitement to a class. Some Trainers will even adjust volume during workouts to push you out of your comfort zone and get the most out of your body, mind, and the exercise you're performing. Playing the latest and greatest music helps motivate our clients.

Classes end with a "finisher": a 5–7-minute sequence of extra-high-intensity exercises with little to no rest. The goal is to really elevate heart rate, increase lactic acid burn, and push the body to its maximum. In most cases, it will be an abdominal sequence. Ending sessions this way allows clients to give that one last push and have a strong and memorable finish. After ending on an endorphin high, clients walk out of the KX studio doors proud, relieved, and ready to tackle the day with a sense of accomplishment.

Ashley Adair, Franchise Partner
KX Pilates Newcastle (NSW)

KX Class, KX Newcastle (NSW)

Whether you're new to reformer workouts or an arabesque aficionado, getting strong and staying that way has never been easier. KX takes the best parts of Pilates and improves upon them. We're more than a fitness routine; we are a lifestyle, a community where everyone is welcome.

THE QUESTION I STILL GET ASKED

"Pilates—is it like yoga?!" People have asked me this question since the beginning of KX and will probably still be asking until the end of time. I can see how yoga and Pilates get placed in the same category, as they are both full body workouts that promote a strong mind-body connection. But when you place yoga and Pilates—especially the KX style—side by side, the differences are apparent.

While some Pilates exercises resemble those used in yoga, the former is more strength-focused, whereas the latter emphasizes breathing, flexibility, and spirituality. Some overlap does exist in all of these areas, but those of us who practice Pilates usually have specific health and fitness goals in mind. Yoga, on the other hand, has more spiritual components attached, for some people at least. If you're looking to get fit, have fun, and challenge yourself by working every muscle in your body, Pilates is an awesome tool. However, when it comes to in-studio workouts, I've learned firsthand that things don't always go according to plan!

BEGINNER BETTY AND QUEEN OF THE QUEEF—TWO VERY DIFFERENT REACTIONS TO WINDY WEATHER

I must have taught thousands of Pilates classes over the years, but my funniest memories come from two separate occasions while I was teaching in London in 2008. The first involved a middle-aged woman in her very first class. For the sake of the story, let's call her Beginner Betty. Betty was quiet and shy from the start, and I did my best to make her feel welcome. She tried to hide herself in the back row of the class, and it seemed that she was giving dynamic Pilates a go to try and kick-start her exercise regime again.

In most beginner classes, I would teach a classic Pilates sequence of exercises called "legs in straps." During this sequence, you lie on your back with each foot in a strap, and, with resistance, perform a combination of hamstring exercises and leg circles. The movements focus on inner thigh, hamstring, and glute strength as well as opening the hips. It's a rather enjoyable and popular sequence that's not too difficult and allows first-time clients to do an exercise they may never have done before, while using the reformer machine to its full extent. At the end of the sequence, we would stretch the inner thighs. With both straps still on each foot, you split your legs out to the sides as far as you can.

Remember, KX Pilates relies on the isolate-fatigue-stretch principle. When you perform the exercise, you isolate the muscle, work it to fatigue, and, finally, stretch it to improve flexibility. During the stretching segments, I would assist clients. I believe that assisted stretching complements the personalized nature of the exercise experience. So, as clients stretched, I went around to each person to help them go that little bit further or take the stretch deeper. In most stretches, assisting would mean a light press on the back, a pull from the arms, or a slight press of the feet. I would usually whisper, "Take a deep breath in, and slowly exhale," and it was on the exhale that I would press. However, with this particular inner thigh stretch, the client is relatively exposed as they lay on their backs with their legs split apart, so I would need to stand almost between their legs and assist by pressing lightly on their inner knees or lower thighs. Due to the delicateness of the position the client was in, it was imperative that you looked into their eyes and NOT down at their crotch.

As I assisted Betty, I was very conscious of trying to make her as comfortable as possible. I got into the assisted stretch position, looked her in the eyes, said "Deep breath in... now exhale." It could not have been timed better. As she exhaled, her body relaxed and, as I pressed her legs down to assist the stretch, out popped an extremely loud fart that the whole class heard. With our eyes still on each other, her facial expression turned to one of shock and disbelief, and we both let out an embarrassed laugh. Her face turned bright red, and I jumped up before I caught a whiff of anything and walked to the other side of the room. The whole class pretended they didn't hear anything, but of course they all did. It was the most uncomfortable three seconds of silence I've ever experienced. I quickly composed myself and finished teaching the class, leaving poor Betty alone. I hope for her sake that she continued along her fitness path, but unfortunately—yet understandably—I never saw Betty again.

A few weeks later, still in London, I was teaching what I thought would be a normal Saturday class. One of the clients was a young European— my guess would be Spanish—girl who was absolutely stunning, with a beautiful accent to match. She seemed very fit and told me she was experienced in Pilates. Her body told me she was telling the truth. And away the class went.

In a similar fashion to the beginner class with Betty, I instructed the legs in straps sequence again. As this class mostly consisted of strong, experienced clients, I added an intermediate twist towards the end of the sequence: a shoulder stand. Still lying on your back, as both feet raise to the ceiling, you use your core to lift your legs and torso up into the shoulder stand, pause at the top, and slowly roll down the spine, articulating one vertebra at a time until the hips touch back down on the reformer carriage once more. This was a great exercise for isolating the core and controlling the body against both resistance and gravity. Plus, it felt cool to perform and, as an instructor, to teach.

As I started correcting a few clients on their technique on the other side of the studio, I heard a giggle coming from the direction of where the Spanish queen was but didn't take much notice. As the repetitions rolled on, the giggling continued. I thought it was strange because she didn't seem to be interacting with the clients either side of her but as I got closer to her and corrected the technique of a client a few machines over, I was intrigued to know what all the fuss was about, so I paid close attention. As she rolled down her spine, I heard what I thought was a fart, and, as her hips touched down, she would giggle. On the next repetition, I heard it again. And then again! I finally clued onto what was going on: as she lifted her body into the shoulder stand, air was getting sucked up into "you know where," only to be expelled when she rolled back down. Where most ladies, I assume, would find this embarrassing and stop the movement, she thought it was hilarious and continued.

When I understood what was going on—and to avoid my own embarrassment—I quickly changed the exercise. Funnily enough, a week later in the same class, she brought her partner in with her. As he checked them both into class, I didn't realize it was the same woman until I cued the shoulder stand into the exercise sequence once more. To my surprise, I heard it happen all over again, but this time she was pointing it out to her partner, and together they were in hysterics. I'd heard the saying, "Couples who train together, stay together," but "Couples who queef together?" That was a new one!

The stories of Beginner Betty and the Spanish Queen of the Queef illustrate just how important mindset is as we attempt to navigate life. How you react to a situation determines whether the event becomes a negative or positive memory. In Beginner Betty's case, she—understandably—reacted with embarrassment and might never have set foot in a Pilates studio again. Whereas the Queen of the Queef embraced the windy weather, realized the comedy potential, and brought an audience for the next session! She definitely knew how to make the best of a potentially awkward moment.

THE CHEEKY STRETCH TEST

"What's the stretch test?"

It's very important to pay attention to what you need to wear to a KX Pilates class. The positions in which certain exercises are performed means different body parts are bending, legs are splitting, and, in frank terms, you are somewhat exposed!

For the men, shorts are great for freedom of movement, BUT bike shorts underneath are a must! Nobody wants anything falling out mid-class. And for the women, again bike shorts or leggings are appropriate to keep everything "down there" out of sight. But for some, what they thought was appropriate attire simply was not.

In around 2011, the Australian compression apparel brand 2XU— pronounced "Two times you"— launched into the fitness scene in Melbourne and, soon after, the world. With lululemon dominating the Pilates and yoga apparel market at the time, 2XU's approach was to focus on the technical aspects of increasing performance and recovery through what they labeled "compression" garments. Originally a running and cycling brand, 2XU and their compression tights became the new activewear trend, and we immediately saw a huge increase in KX clientele wearing their gear.

But little did people know that they were not made for Pilates classes! Looking at yourself in the mirror, there was no issue but when the fabric stretched, it became see-through. Most of the time when the client had her butt in the air or her legs split apart, she didn't have the right viewpoint to notice what was happening—but we Trainers certainly did. As you could imagine, I have seen it all. The color of ladies' underwear all the way to ladies who wore no underwear at all!

Now I'm a pretty straight shooter, and for my whole life I have held the view that if I were in the same situation, I would like to know. Over the years, I have gotten used to uncomfortable conversations with friends and family. If you had something in your teeth, I would (quietly) let you know. If there was someone that needed deodorant or chewing gum, I would quietly let them know. But this was a bit different! Telling a client (even quietly) that their leggings are see-through is embarrassing for both sides: embarrassing for the client for obvious reasons but embarrassing for me, too, as I'm telling them after clearly witnessing and observing them in class for almost an hour. So, I needed a way to communicate the problem politely and effectively in a more informative and less embarrassing way— so I came up with the "stretch test."

The stretch test is simple. You stand with your back towards a mirror and your feet shoulder width apart. While keeping your legs long, you then simply bend over to touch your toes and look through your legs in the mirror at your bum and legs. This position will stretch the fabric—similar to what I'd see in class—and now you are in a position to see whether your leggings are see-through or not.

The conversation then became more subtle. "Hey, have you done the stretch test in those leggings yet? If not, perhaps you should." Once I explained, they'd either understand where I was coming from or quickly go into the change rooms for privacy and do it themselves to find out the answer. It even carried through to stores that sold activewear as the test you'd perform pre-purchase, pressuring companies that have "yoga and Pilates" retail lines to make sure the clothing wasn't see-through. So, my question is—have you done the cheeky stretch test on all of your leggings? Or has your trainer been copping an eyeful?

LESSONS LEARNED

1. Pressure and necessity can cause innovation. Joseph Pilates could have spent his imprisonment feeling sorry for himself but instead chose to invent a whole new fitness regime! When you're in a tough situation, considering what you CAN do is much more useful than considering what you CAN'T.

2. How we react to an event determines whether it is positive or negative. When something embarrassing happens, we can choose to feel humiliated or, instead, find humor in the situation.

3. Whenever you try on a new piece of activewear, always perform the cheeky stretch test—no exceptions!

"If there is no struggle,
there is no progress."

—Frederick Douglass

Chapter 4

THE SECRET INGREDIENT TO OUR SUCCESS

After my time in London, I was pumped to start on what was to become KX Pilates.

I landed back in Australia only to find that I was $20,000 in debt to my father. For the whole time I was away, he had been kindly paying off my travel credit card when the statements came through, and let's just say we were both surprised when we added up the total. The excitement of being home quickly passed, and I was hit with a huge reality check that opening a Pilates studio was still out of reach. I was twenty-six years old, in debt, single, living with my parents again, and driving my dad's car.

I returned to bar and gaming work in a pokies venue, a role I'd escaped only a few years prior. For three months, I was back to dealing with the local riffraff and being in a depressing environment. This was not how I had envisaged life in Melbourne would be for me upon my return!

So, I pitched my idea to the one person I knew would listen—my father. I explained everything: the concept behind personalized boutique fitness, the style of Pilates that I had learned, and how much I thought it was all going to cost. I had even drafted up a very shabby business plan to prove to him how serious I was. Although my father was a businessman himself, he was not a man who took many risks, and I do not doubt that my pitch seemed like a big one. But he immediately saw the passion in my eyes, and the next thing I knew, I was in his bank manager's office signing my first business loan, which my father had guaranteed, for $120,000. My father, the man who had already taught me so much, was again extending his hand. He was the second person to believe in my vision.

Now, it was go-time! I had $120,000 of someone else's money, and I would use every dollar to bring my dream to life. It was actually happening. I had a name, but I needed a logo, so I called up an old friend of mine, Jeffrey, more affectionately known as "Jeffa." Jeffa and I met when we were six years old. We went through primary and secondary school together and for as long as I can remember, he always had an incredible knack with a pencil. He used to draw the coolest stuff for me, and my bedroom wall growing up had a constant array of Jeffa's artwork of army men, superheroes, and sports stars. As he grew into an adult, not surprisingly, he became a brilliant graphic designer. By day, Jeffa was (and still is) a senior designer at Ford Automotive and heads up the Australasian interior design team. If you drive a Ford, the chances are that he and his team designed your interior. But by night, he would turn into the KX designer, working out of his bedroom in his parents' house! Concept after concept, color after color, I kept sending him back to the drawing board. The two letters I had chosen, K and X, were so incredibly difficult to design that he would constantly curse them. But then, he got it.

Before he showed me, he got the tick of approval from all the designers on his team at Ford, so he knew he was onto something. Although we broke almost every typical rule in the art of logo design, we loved it. It symbolized just how cool this company was going to be.

The original KX Logo

I had the bank loan, and I had the logo. Therefore, the search was on for the first KX Pilates studio location. It wasn't long until I found the location in the affluent inner-city Melbourne suburb of Malvern. Everything about it was perfect: it was located next to a Coles supermarket, there was ample parking, and it was on the first floor, which kept the rent down. It was also on the iconic eastern suburbs high street shopping strip of Glenferrie Road, which everyone in Melbourne knew. The landlord saw my amateur nature a mile away, and the lease terms were ridiculously in their favor. The security deposit I paid was double anything else on the market. They played the "take it or leave it" scenario, and I took it. But the site was perfect, so it wasn't long before I signed the lease and construction began. I know better now and have since learned to negotiate.

The first KX Pilates studio opened its doors on February 26, 2010. Woo-hoo! Or so I thought. I would like to say that it was also the first day of trading, but with my lack of experience, zero business acumen, and my obsession with getting the studio looking as perfect as possible, I hadn't done any marketing or pre-sales to get people in the door. So, on my very first day of opening, not one person walked in! It was a lonely day, let me assure you, but I was in a positive mood. I had started my journey as a business owner. With the excitement of my new venture, I invited all of my friends and family in for free sessions, started pounding the pavement doing mailbox drops, advertised in local newspapers, and visited local businesses, getting to know them and creating a real community feel around the studio.

Trying to differentiate this new fitness style meant educating people. Most women didn't know the difference between traditional Pilates and the dynamic version I had introduced and had only done mat Pilates at their local gym. They were not familiar with a Pilates reformer machine at all.

But I was on a mission to make a name for myself, for KX, and for dynamic Pilates.

Constantly informing and educating people was key to that mission and by far the greatest challenge. With numbers slowly growing each week and word-of-mouth spreading across Melbourne, I kept doing what I was good at: providing an exceptional fitness experience. I just wanted to see my clients smile and I knew if that was happening, I was heading in the right direction.

Starting KX Pilates was hard going because, in addition to it being a new business, I had to pioneer an entirely new fitness concept. At the time, most men had no idea what Pilates was. "No, it is nothing like yoga!" I repeated constantly.

After a few weeks, the excitement died down, and the grind began. I'll be honest; I had no idea how to run a business. I had no idea what a profit and loss statement was, and I had to teach myself how to write up an invoice. I hardly knew how to use internet banking properly—but I would learn.

At the end of each month, I sat down and did the books with my father, and although it was my least favorite thing in the world, I would learn. Was it hard work, repetitive and monotonous at times? Yes, but I could see the light at the end of the tunnel, so I stuck it out.

With only myself and two other Trainers, I was working 60–80 hours a week, which consisted of 40 classes, 5–8 private sessions, all of the administration, phone calls, and emails, and marketing as much as I could in between all of that. At that stage, I booked everyone into classes via an Excel spreadsheet and took reservations in the studio or by phone. I'd be up at 4:30 am every morning and home most nights after 10 pm once I had cleaned the studio ready for the next day. But work didn't stop when I got home. With Mom's help, I would wash, dry, and fold all of the sweat towels ready for the next day. It was tough going.

KX Pilates Malvern (VIC) reception 2010

I was still living with my parents and driving my father's car. At that stage, I'd even had KX Pilates decals put on Dad's car, trying everything possible to get the KX name out there. For the first twelve months, I was only paying myself $200 per week and went super lean on my studio fit out. The glass reception table and chair were on loan from my sister's dining table collection, and the studio reception was made up of her living room couch and her coffee table that I borrowed from storage. With no money for uniforms, I frequently donned an adidas Originals three-stripe tracksuit and a t-shirt. It wasn't perfect, but it was enough for me to get by and pull off an amateur boutique feel in the studio.

Due to the hours I worked, my social life was non-existent, which was just as well because I quit drinking for a while. I couldn't afford to go out, and I also hated dealing with the alcohol-induced anxiety and depression hangover that came after. My London days of drinking to excess had put a toll on my body and mind, and I needed to give it up to keep a strong, positive mindset and stay motivated. I would train every day, and my diet was perfect. Healthy body, healthy mind. I needed to stay focused, and, being the face of this brand, I also needed to keep fit.

It wasn't easy. Although I tried as hard as I could to stay positive, there wasn't a day that went by in those early months where I didn't want to quit. I felt very alone.

During this time, both my grandmother and grandfather on my father's side passed away. They were married for more than fifty years when they died. Both over ninety, my grandparents were in the same nursing home when we watched my grandmother slowly lose her battle with dementia. My grandfather had promised her father on their wedding day to always look after her, so, when she passed, he had no further reason to live and died only three weeks later. Their ashes were buried in the church's rose garden where they were married, just one street away from the Malvern studio. They were close by and no doubt watching over me.

My parents were really supportive during this time. Mom always had dinner waiting for me when I got home, and they were always there to support and encourage me to keep persisting. Dad would often stay up and wait for me to get home. He wanted to hear how my day had been and share stories of when he first started in business and how difficult it was for him. This provided me with much-needed comfort. He would remind me that all of the hard work was worth it and nothing easy was ever worth doing. Sound words of advice that still hold to this day. I also felt like I had to prove it to myself and them for believing in me and helping me get the much-needed loan that enabled me to follow my dreams.

Peter and Dianne Smith AKA Mom and Dad.
KX Port Melbourne (VIC) Launch Party 2011

LIKE-MINDED PEOPLE

In May 2010, three months after opening my first studio, the initial excitement of launching KX Pilates wore off. I was lonely. I started to seek business groups where I could mix with like-minded individuals. I tried a few local community groups, but they all seemed to be filled with people over fifty who were either lawyers or accountants and had never even heard of Pilates! Boring and far from inspiring.

A friend recommended a seminar for young entrepreneurs called The Entourage Unconvention, where I met founder Jack Delosa and his best friend, Andrew Morello. A start-up as well, The Entourage aimed to be Australia's leading educator and community of young entrepreneurs. I had found my place! I was surrounded by start-up businesses struggling just as much as I was but had owners with the passion and drive to succeed. They were innovative millennials who tested the waters in new markets with new products. The networking was invaluable, and I was highly impressed.

At the end of that seminar, I signed up for the two-day intensive course. Here, I had to draw up an outline of KX and explain what we did, what our vision was, and how and when we would exit. Today, I still have the slideshow I created that outlines the goal of ten company studios, fifty franchises, and to exit by 2020. I've had that goal in the back of my mind ever since, although I still question whether I could fully exit this business. This company is too much a part of me.

After the course, I was so enthused about learning more that I signed up for their then twelve-month Scalable and Saleable (S&S) program. A week later, I was in a room with Jack, Morello, and nine other people. These guys were twenty-two years old at the time but absolute guns at business, and I was immediately impressed. What I learned from them and the help and guidance they provided no doubt kick-started the initial success of KX. We were their first S&S group in Melbourne and, with only six businesses in the group, it was easy for us to meet monthly in the back of Morello's brother's real estate agency in Flemington, picking each other's brains and discussing all of the issues we were facing day-to-day in our businesses. I was a sponge and implemented almost everything I learned, from referral programs and building strategic partnerships to gaining corporate sponsorships and building a following. This community was the turning point for my business. I was also lucky enough to have monthly coaching sessions with Stuart Cook, the then-CEO of Mexican fast-food franchise Zambrero, another young gun who guided me through the whole franchise process later down the track.

With this support and knowledge behind me, I felt unstoppable, and I was confident that my dreams would become a reality. As I wrote to Jack a few years later: "The Entourage has not taught me to dream. I did that on my own. Rather, it has taught me how exactly to go about achieving my dreams. The steps to action and an environment where succeeding is the norm."

At the end of 2019, we had twelve company studios, fifty-two franchise studios in Australia, and our first international studio in Jakarta, Indonesia. My initial goal I wrote down in 2010 with the Entourage had been achieved!

Although the first year may have been a struggle, traction was starting to build, and KX had begun to make a buzz in Melbourne's fitness scene. KX also attracted clients and friends who knew we were onto something and loved the direction the business was moving in. As the saying goes, "behind every great man is an even more amazing woman." In my case, it turned out it was "women," plural. The dating game for me in the first year was non-existent.

It's not the founder but the brand followers who create a movement.

Saying that you earn basically nothing and still live with your parents is not enticing to the ladies. But, in 2010, a few months after opening KX,

Andrea Fiorenza—or more affectionately known as Andi—came into my life. We met at a mutual friend's thirtieth birthday, and I was lucky enough to sit next to her. As party tricks were shared and laughing escalated, our conversation just seemed so easy and natural. It wasn't long before we realized that many of my clients were her work colleagues.

Incredibly gorgeous, with the most amazing smile I had ever seen, she was also straight to the point, didn't put up with bullshit, and seemed extremely genuine. So, immediately we hit it off, and our friendship blossomed. As our friendship grew, so did her support. A great KX advocate, she would constantly bring her friends to try a class and helped get the KX name out in her networks. She would help me wash towels—I think there may be a running theme here relating to how much I hate washing towels—and turned out to be a great sounding board, offering wise advice from her years of marketing experience in a big corporation.

The time came when I realized I wanted more from our relationship. I built up the courage to ask her out on a date and, before we had even ordered our entrées, I confidently explained to her how everything in my life was going exceptionally well with work and family. Still, something was missing, someone to share it with: her. In my head, I had utterly nailed my "courting speech," but, to my surprise, with a flattered smile on her face, she politely said "no thanks." I then had to sit through the entire dinner and movie with rejection all over my face. Ahh, the embarrassment! But, to my delight, two days later she called me up and told me that she had made a mistake. We have been together ever since.

Andi was the third person who truly believed in my vision, and it's her incredible love, support, and hard work that has helped us get KX to where it is today. So much so that this business is now "ours." With Andi by my side, I have always felt like I could achieve anything. Not only could I now work even harder to grow KX, but I had someone to share it with and have fun with along the way. Eighteen months later, she quit her job and came to work as KX's first marketing and operations manager. Although her salary in those early years was a quarter of what she'd earned in her previous corporate role, it never bothered her, as she was in love with the business just as much as I was. And I'm happy to share that she has never looked back.

If I was the founder/CEO (at the time), growing the business and connecting the dots, Andi was the unnamed COO, the workhorse behind the scenes, ensuring that everything was organized, systemized, and executed correctly. From marketing manager to growing a team as head of marketing and systems specialist, she now sits on both internal and external advisory boards. She is still probably the one person that knows this business inside out, more so than me.

Looking back to when we were involved so heavily in the business, we had an incredible journey, moving to New South Wales for two years to start the flagship Sydney studio in Surry Hills and then on to Brisbane for a few months to assist Franchise Partners there. After countless trips to Bali to host KX Retreats and before returning home to Melbourne, we settled to have our beautiful children, Archer Jack, Ava Charlotte, and

Andi Fiorenza

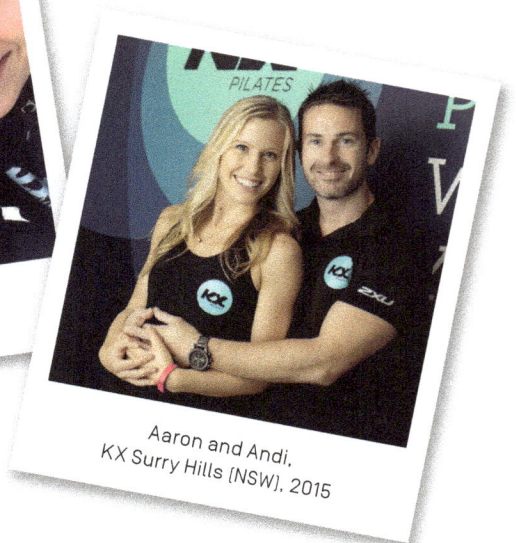

Aaron and Andi,
KX Surry Hills (NSW), 2015

Amelia Willow, solidifying our "A-Team." Between getting engaged on Whitehaven Beach in the Whitsundays in 2016 and eloping at the top of the snow-capped Vail Mountain in Colorado in 2018, we had countless other adventures.

I am just in awe of her, being by my side, assisting, and forever supporting our roller coaster life during those years. The success of KX is very much due to the hard work she has put in since its inception, loving and growing this brand and our family, but, most importantly, making me look good at the same time!

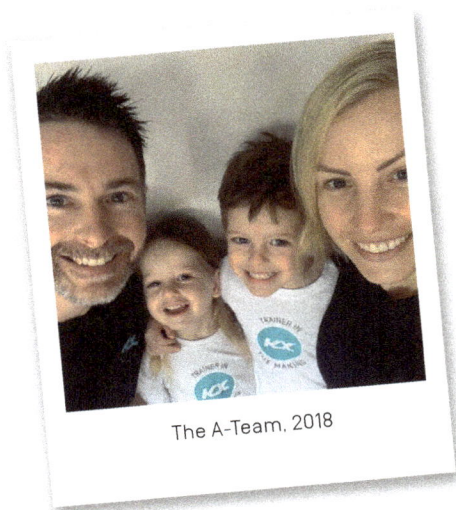

The A-Team, 2018

I MENTIONED THERE WAS MORE THAN ONE WOMAN, RIGHT?

When the first studio in Malvern was still in its start-up phase, it began to achieve great success. Instead of waiting to self-fund the second studio, I used its success to convince my bank manager to loan me more money. In August 2011, our second studio opened in Port Melbourne. This studio proved that I was onto something big with KX and enabled me to bring three extraordinary women into my life.

The backbone of this company is our KX Academy and Training Department, and the backbone of the training department is Amie Skinner. I initially met Amie in London on my first teacher training day at

Bootcamp Pilates, and we immediately hit it off. A Pilates guru for years, Amie was one of Bootcamp's strongest and most popular trainers, juggling her time between teaching Pilates, personal training, and jetsetting off to France to head up corporate leadership retreats. After I left Bootcamp,

Amie Skinner

we kept in touch, but it wasn't until she visited Australia on holiday in 2010 that I told her of my plans for KX and how she would need to be there when the second studio opened.

Like so many, Amie fell in love with Australia. So, when I opened in Port Melbourne, she jumped at the opportunity to move to Melbourne and start her new life with KX. As studio manager, Amie developed our first "official" KX Training Academy, getting it accredited with AUSactive (formally Fitness Australia) and achieving a high standard of training throughout the company. She became State Training Manager and is now Head of Training, overseeing both national and international training departments. So much of our solid training foundation is thanks to Amie.

In late 2015, she left KX to purchase her own independent Pilates studio, as owning her own studio was an itch she always needed to scratch, and there were no available KX studios available to open in the locations she wanted. As a result, our quality of training suffered. Twelve months later, I sat her down and asked her to come back. As much as she loved having her own studio, I think deep down she missed being a part of a company that was ingrained in her DNA just as much as we missed her.

In 2017 we converted her studio to a **KX** studio, and she rejoined the family to head up the training department once more. Three months after converting her studio to **KX**, her revenue increased by 300 percent, so her decision was one we were both grateful for and just another example of the power of being in a franchise network and known brand. Amie has since sold her studio back to the company to run so one hundred percent of her focus can be on the national training department and now on the international front. We are just so grateful to have her as part of our Senior Leadership Team.

In 2011, Eli Censor was a trainer in the second **KX** Academy group that Amie ever taught for the Port Melbourne studio. Apart from being a great instructor, Eli was a natural at connecting with people. She immediately saw potential in the **KX** name and brand, and it was only a few months later that she sat me down and asked about opening her own studio. Not having the franchise side of the company set up yet, we decided on a partnership arrangement for the next three **KX** studios where I would build and open the studios, and she would run them. A perfect fit, as the day-to-day running of studios was no longer my passion, and she absolutely loved and excelled at it. I loved building studios and getting everything ready for launch and then when the doors opened, I was happy to pass on the baton to Eli.

Six months later, in June 2012, Eli and I opened a **KX** studio in Richmond. It was a success from the beginning, showing profit in just four weeks.

Eli Censor at KX Richmond (VIC) Launch Party, July 2012

Not only did Eli have an amazing network of people she brought to KX, but the KX name was starting to build a following in Melbourne. Instead of people asking, "What is KX Pilates?" it was more like, "How awesome is it that KX Pilates is now opening near me?!"

Our partnership was thriving. From the beginning, we laid out expectations and knew exactly what our roles were and to this day, we have an extremely healthy business relationship coupled with a great friendship. Not only did Eli believe in my vision from the beginning, but she was also my first follower in business who put her money on the line and risked it all on what was still only a start-up. With Eli running these studios, I focused on the legal framework, franchise documentation, getting KX systemized, and business growth. Our partnership studios two and three were just as successful and in the years preceding, I sold Eli my share of the businesses so she could thrive on her own. Eli is still a valued and successful multi-site KX Franchise Partner with one of the highest portfolios of studios in the KX network. A fantastic example of timing, risk, and hard work that has well and truly paid off.

In his book *Good to Great,* author Jim Collins stresses the importance of seating the right people with the right attitude on the right bus. If those people are not suitable for your business or brand or aren't headed in the same direction, kick them off. I've also learned to put the right people in the right seats as well. Sometimes all it takes is a little juggling to get people in the right place to enable them to realize their full potential.

LESSONS LEARNED

1. Nothing worth doing is ever easy. Starting a business will be one of the biggest roller coasters in your life. But it's one of the best decisions you will ever make and is all worth it in the end.

2. Create measurable goals and have a vision. Share this vision with your followers so you can help support each other along the journey. Reward your first follower(s) and hold them close. They took a risk on you and without them, the movement would never have begun.

3. When asked for the top three things that helped his business succeed, Richard Branson nominated, "People, people, and people." I agree, but I'd also go one step further and say it's the relationships with key people that attributed to OUR success.

PART.TWO

THE
EVOLUTION
OF KX

"Good business
leaders create a vision,
articulate the vision,
passionately own the vision,
and relentlessly drive it
to completion."

—Jack Welch

Chapter 5

TO SEE IS TO BELIEVE: FROM VISION TO REALITY

I saw firsthand that, in gyms, hitting sales targets was more important than providing a personalized approach. KX was going to be a better way of doing fitness.

I felt like I could make a real difference and have a positive impact on the fitness industry. I also wanted to capture the idea that the local community members could support each other in their fitness journey and create a sense of belonging.

As a KX client, you feel like you belong to something more than just a local Pilates studio. The bigger KX community was a larger group of like-minded individuals who were all on the same path to success in their lives. Through my business learnings, I realized that KX could be so much more than a fitness studio. It was becoming a movement of people that were heading in the same direction and could support each other on the way. KX became a way of life.

I still remember my father looking at my financial figures for the first three studios and asking why I would want to keep going. To him, the money coming in was enough to support a good lifestyle. For me, it was never about the money. I wanted to create something amazing and for people to experience the "KX difference." I wanted to create a brand that people were proud to be involved with and recognized as premium.

WHEN VISITING OTHER BUSINESSES, I ALWAYS ASKED, "WHY?"

Why have membership options with lock-in contracts? Why would you force people to pay you when they don't come? Why do studios only have a three-month validity for session packs and not extend when you ask kindly? Why, why, why? But the answer I would always come to was: because of the money businesses could earn at the end of the day. They always chose dollars over the customer and the experience. I wanted to put our clients before profits.

Before KX, when I was failing in my nutritional start-up, I attended a conference in Vegas where the late Jim Rohn was the keynote speaker. His words of wisdom?

"Care more about your customers than you do about the money you will make from them, and you will be successful."

This stuck with me.

I had that view from the very beginning with KX; clients were always going to be put first, and that's how I knew we couldn't fail. As KX grew bigger and better, I constantly implemented new company policies based on my reflections and a rejection of my pet hates.

I didn't want any lock-in contracts. To this day, seventy-five percent of people who own gym memberships do not make the most of them. From a business perspective, locking someone in to pay or charging them exorbitant fees to cancel plays on the ups and downs of human motivation and to me, it was daylight robbery. So, similar to Bootcamp Pilates in London, KX runs on session packs. "Pay for when you come, not for when you don't." We have monthly packs for clients who come regularly, and you are not obliged to buy that pack again unless you want to, as we understand that circumstances change. No lock-in contracts also means accountability. Our job is to impress our clients every single time they walk into the studio so they want to come back time and time again. We can't have "off" days, and we can never get complacent. We also have session packs that are valid for twelve months. When I was a client of other fitness brands, I was sick of losing sessions when my circumstances changed. People go away; they become unmotivated; life happens. But make it easy for them to come back, and they will.

We also offered access to water fountains, sweat towels, delicious apples, and beautiful natural oils to make the studio smell amazing.

Unfortunately, in 2020, COVID-19 changed the rules, and we had to stop providing apples and towels. Hopefully, one day, we can bring these back.

All of these things helped create a unique experience. Even the ten-minute gap between classes was significant. Not only is a fifty-minute, high-intensity class much more appealing than a one-hour session, but the ten minutes between classes was perfect for giving clients time to ask questions and provide feedback. At the same time, Trainers had time to connect with clients on a personal level. All of these things were invaluable in creating the right experience.

WHEN PURPOSE BECOMES REALITY

My time in boutique fitness companies overseas showed me that I had to tackle the growth of KX differently.

The studios in London stayed company-owned, and I had not seen any business grow to more than six studios. I had witnessed many business leads who wanted their own studios. Generally, they were either trainers or clients who had already fallen in love with the style, brand, and business model, and owning a studio seemed like the next step in their career development.

I saw firsthand that all of the initial trainers who started with me at Bootcamp wanted to either buy into the business or open a new partnership studio, only to be turned away by the owner. This led to the obvious: they started their own studios and became the competition. I knew there was a better way to capture these ambassadors and use them to the business's advantage.

IGNITING MY PASSION FOR FRANCHISING

This was about the time my focus and passion became crystal clear. I knew how to get the best out of people, and I wanted to help them achieve their goals and reach their full potential. I wanted to change lives for the better.

I realized that I could combine my love of business with helping people. I would franchise KX Pilates.

Franchising came with its own set of challenges. The franchise world was, and still is, a fascinating one. There are many different franchise models, but the most common involves obtaining an upfront franchise fee and taking an ongoing royalty or support fees. Locations would also usually provide a small contribution—generally between 2–4 percent—of revenue for the national marketing fund to spend on collective marketing efforts and national advertising and campaigns. The initial fee provides access to intellectual property and the license to operate under that brand for a given time (e.g., 5–10 years). Also included is a step-by-step start-up guide—or franchise manual—which explains exactly how to set up the business, all the trade secrets, look books, fit out guides, brand guidelines, preferred suppliers, and, in our case, the KX Academy training process.

There is a saying in the franchise world that you don't make money from the initial sale, but you do when you build solid, long-term relationships with your franchise partners. Help them achieve greatness, and the royalties will follow. It's pretty simple: they succeed; you succeed.

In fitness, all you have is your reputation. The same goes for business in general. You can spend years building a good reputation and ruin it in seconds with one poor choice. Doing things the wrong way will also get you in the media for the wrong reasons.

I wanted to make KX different!

And I was going to disrupt the franchise world in the process. I set a goal to always do right by the brand, our staff, and our Franchise Partners and to stay ethical and be contactable at any time. Whatever was happening or whoever was running this business in the future, my door would always be open.

DEFINING KX

My vision was clear: bring the KX experience to every corner of Australia, and the franchising model was going to help me achieve it.

In 2012, after successfully opening three studios, I was having a coffee with a good friend of mine, Daz, who asked me what my dreams for KX and the company were.

At the time, Daz was a senior brand developer and was also the co-founder of a successful tech start-up. With a great big smile on my face, I told him all of my grand plans. Daz did not return my smile. In his most polite voice, he said that, in his professional opinion, for KX to grow, it needed a new, stronger brand and identity. "What was that, Daz?" I was utterly offended! The KX logo was like my baby, and I had a huge personal connection to it. I immediately

Remember the friend's thirtieth birthday where Andi and I met? Well, it was Daz's wife Hinda's birthday that day. Daz and Hinda are both great friends that Andi and I became close with before we even knew each other, and it was Hinda's birthday that brought us together for the first time. Why mention Hinda? You'll understand a little later.

dismissed his comments; he had only been into a KX studio once—for a launch party—and had never actually done the KX workout. At the time, he wasn't even a fitness enthusiast—what did he know?

Twelve months later, we had just opened studio five, with number six on the way. It was the beginning of a big year. The process of franchising KX was underway, and I again found myself in a café chatting to Daz. He stressed how much I needed to focus on the brand if I wanted to take KX around Australia.

This time, I listened, and, instead of dismissing his comments, I realized that Daz was right. Everything he was saying was true: KX didn't have a *brand*; it had a logo. We had not defined what KX really was. We had no brand guidelines or style guides, nor did we have brand messaging or even a basic tagline. I knew in my head what the company values were, but I had never formalized them. My lack of business experience was starting to shine through once more, and I finally realized that even with studio six just about to open, we were still amateurs. We shook hands on a price, and the KX Pilates rebrand began.

The rebrand took around six months and was incredibly difficult. There was a lot of push-pull, and it was tough to separate myself from what I had grown to love, but I was forced to look at the bigger picture. Daz taught me a hell of a lot about branding in that short amount of time. A brand is more than a logo; it is the feeling. Whenever a client walks into a studio, visits our website, connects with a trainer, or

Our first rebrand, 2013

sees any brand touchpoint, they get a feeling. It's how they are greeted and treated. It's also your reputation, what you are known for.

I did push back on major changes to the logo that Jeffa had so carefully designed four years prior, so Daz cleaned it up, dropped the cursive "Pilates" text, and wrapped it in a circle to bring balance.

The next big thing to re-evaluate was our name.

KX had always been pronounced "kicks" by the internal team and long-standing clients. I even used to correct people when they called it "K-X." Initially, I believed it was good to have a sense of exclusivity, where only people close to the brand knew how to pronounce our name correctly. The "if you know, you know" mentality. But in the branding world, if people cannot pronounce your name correctly, you are in trouble from the start. If we were only going to open a few studios, maybe we would have kept it like that. The problem with "kicks" was that it had no meaning behind it, and, if we were to expand across Australia, we needed it to.

We issued client surveys as part of a mission to research this, and I soon found out that everyone called us K-X. The confusion needed to stop. But first, we had to define the meaning behind K and X, two incredibly difficult letters to work with. Drawing on my drive to help others and continuously improve, the Kaizen Xperience presented itself. Japanese for "change for the better" or "continuous improvement," *kaizen* was not only a philosophy that defined who we were perfectly, but it also defined who I was personally. We were always seeking to improve not only as a company but as individuals in everyday life.

Next, we developed the Company Vision.

TO PROVIDE A PERSONALIZED
BOUTIQUE FITNESS EXPERIENCE
THAT PEOPLE WILL LOVE,
BOTH IN AUSTRALIA AND BEYOND

There are some powerful words in that statement.

"**Personalized**" is what KX and our small class sizes are all about. Clients will always be their own person and never a number at KX.

We are not just a workout, but an entire "**Fitness experience**" at every touchpoint with our clients.

The word "**Boutique**" brings its own standard of professionalism and sophistication, showing that we are made up of many boutique offerings, although we're a bigger company.

And of course, the big one, "**LOVE**." I don't just want people to like KX but LOVE what we do, who we are, and what we stand for.

This affinity with the brand makes people feel like they belong and will keep them coming back time and time again.

The real purpose of this company had now been brought to the surface.

WE CHANGE LIVES FOR THE BETTER

My purpose, our purpose, at KX is quite simple. "WE CHANGE LIVES FOR THE BETTER." That's the meaning behind why we jump out of bed in the morning, why we tackle the endless challenges that business throws at us and ride the highs and lows. That's why we are in this game. Don't get me wrong, profits are nice. But remember what the late Jim Rohn taught me: care more about your customers than the money you will make from them.

There's simply nothing more rewarding than seeing the positive influence we have on the lives of our clients each and every day. We get to see people leave the studio smiling and in a better state of mind than when they walked in. And this is just the beginning. We have worked with clients over weeks, months, and years to help them define themselves and reach their potential both in the studio and in other areas of their lives. The positive influence we have on people's lives is the FUEL that drives this business.

Let's dive into the details of what "WE CHANGE LIVES FOR THE BETTER" means to me, why we do what we do, and why we are still so passionate about KX Pilates after a decade in the industry.

Who are "WE?"—Andi and I, our CEO and the HQ Team, our Franchise Partners, our Trainers, our Partnerships, and our Suppliers.

What kind of "CHANGE?"—We make a positive difference and generate smiles, happiness, and appreciation. We give people's lives meaning and purpose and provide physical connection through touch and tactile cueing. Physical and mental change.

Whose "LIVES?"—Our clients, PLUS everyone included in the "WE" field above. We all help change each other's lives.

What is "BETTER?"—We provide value, improvement, purpose, confidence, energy, belonging, significance, and human connection.

Our Vision may be "to provide a personalized boutique fitness experience that people will LOVE," but it's our purpose of "we change lives for the better" that keeps us going. Clients may come for the workout, but they stay because they soon belong to our family, and KX becomes a valued part of their lives. When we reach this goal as a company, we become TIMELESS. And that's where the longevity in the KX business lies.

New client by new client, class by class, trainer by trainer, employee by employee, Franchise Partner by Franchise Partner, it's truly humbling that the outcome of our purpose has been not only the growth of the individuals we have touched, but the reach we now have and continue to expand.

Our reach now spans oceans, cultures, and languages. "We change lives for the better" has gone international, and the goal of global reach is at the forefront of our minds. We take comfort in knowing that no matter our country, culture, religion, or gender, we are all equal, and we can all share this same purpose.

Then came the creation of brand messaging. This would help us communicate to our clients, articulate what our brand stands for, what it promises, and how to express our vision. It forms a larger cohesive story to help position the business in our clients' minds. Many companies' biggest mistake is having their tagline explain what they do or sell when it should be more than that.

Thus, the KX tagline was born: **DEFINE YOURSELF**.

The tagline works perfectly with the kaizen way of "small and ongoing improvement" and "changing for the better." It can also have a different meaning to everyone, be personalized easily, and go quite deep, to wherever an individual wants to take it. You can define your vision of where you are and where you are going. You can define your purpose in life. It can be as simple as defining your body on a physical front, or it can be something more complex. It is whatever you make of it. But one thing holds true: those words have meaning and power.

Next, we articulated the KX Mission.

This central message explains what KX does and what value we create for clients. It combines a direct description of our business with our brand purpose:

TO EMPOWER PEOPLE TO ACHIEVE THEIR GOALS AND REACH THEIR FULL POTENTIAL.

The KX mission had a very personal aspect to it. From an early age, helping people achieve their full potential was my passion and why I got into the fitness industry. I always tried to help people and wanted to encapsulate the team and brand in the "we" aspect of the business. It was no longer about me and what I had done but about the fantastic individuals behind this brand helping clients be the best versions of themselves every day.

To bring our mission to life, we developed supporting messages and performed a survey across the entire network, from Trainers to clients. The results were clear. There were four main reasons why our clients kept coming back to KX: the KX workout, the buzzing atmosphere of our studios, our excellent Trainers, and the ease of our online systems.

The following messages capture how we help our clients, through our workouts, Trainers, systems, and studios.

TONED UP AND CONFIDENCE BOOSTING
OUR WORKOUT WILL PUSH YOU TO GET THERE

PUMPED UP AND BARRIER BREAKING
OUR TRAINERS WILL SUPPORT YOU TO GET THERE

EASY PLANNING AND SIMPLE SCHEDULING
OUR ONLINE SYSTEMS WILL ENSURE YOU GET THERE

A WELCOMING AND BUZZING ATMOSPHERE
OUR STUDIOS WILL INSPIRE YOU TO GET THERE

Now that we had sorted the things of importance on the outside, it was time to look internally at our culture and values. Our company values are guiding principles of behavior for all of us. They directly affect how we interact with each other, our clients, Franchise Partners, and suppliers. They are the backbone of how we hire and evaluate our people and how partnerships are formed. At KX, we value relationships, positivity, innovation, and proactivity. These four elements capture how we want KX, both the business and our people, to behave.

THE KX VALUES

1. Respectful Relationships

Professional. Treat others the way we would want to be treated. Clients, Employees, and Franchise Partners are all equal. Everyone is on the same level. No one is better than you, yet you are no better than anyone else. Stay professional and always be polite.

KX Pilates Surry Hills (NSW), 2015

KX Pilates Mornington (VIC), 2014

2. Vibrant Positivity

Having a crack at it and giving it a go. Outgoing attitude. Being optimistic, no matter what the situation. Living life to its fullest. Going out of your way to impress. Enjoying yourself and everyone around you. Having a good time while you work. And most of all, make it FUN!

3. Above and Beyond

Go further, each and every time. Proactivity. Taking ownership. Constantly trying to exceed expectations becomes the norm. Aim to consistently surprise and delight. No attitude.

4. Evolution Through Innovation

A belief in progression and improvement. Constantly making things better, physically and mentally. Learning never stops. Fail forward. To make mistakes is to be human and is acceptable and necessary to grow and develop.

I wanted to build a culture that helped attract good talent.

KX is all about the people: building relationships, getting fitter, and seeing results together. We keep the boutique fitness feeling but maintain professionalism at all times. Have a question? Feel free to ask. Have feedback? Feel free to give it. When you contact us, you know that you will speak to a real person who cares, and your query will be answered. Through our local benefits program, you get to meet and know local businesses in your community and gain offers and discounts just for being a KX client.

We also created guidelines by which everyone in the business is measured. Firstly, they must be fit, health-conscious individuals who take pride in their appearance. Clients need to be motivated by their Trainers and look up to them. They are vibrant, bubbly, energetic, passionate, professional, and have confidence and belief in the KX brand. They also need to have a strong work ethic with an informal and playful approach, be helpful, patient, and capable of providing the KX experience.

And if we were asking all of the above from our staff, we knew we had to give back. We introduced twelve-month loyalty bonuses, quarterly training days, and annual conferences to upskill and engage our people, as well as regular social days where we could all let our hair down and have fun. We wanted to grow the bond and make our staff feel special to be a part of KX, so we also included staff members of the quarter and year awards to put people on a pedestal for the rest of the network and publicly congratulate them on their achievements. In the beginning, our churn rate was too high for my liking. But once all these points were implemented and we shifted focus to company culture and smarter recruitment, we lost very few people. We also put additional focus into the KX Academy. Our KX Trainers provide the dynamic, personalized experience that our clients keep coming back for. Every studio has a real sense of community, and our amazing team of Trainers is such a big part of that. We realized that our Trainers were so much more than just trainers.

THE DIFFERENT ROLES OUR KX TRAINERS PLAY—THEY'RE MORE THAN JUST TRAINERS

1. MOOD CHANGER

I firmly believe in the power a **KX Trainer** has to change the moods of their clients. No matter how our clients walk through the door or how their day has gone (good or bad), it is our role to make sure they walk out feeling incredible. It's also about more than just getting a good workout; they crack a joke, have a laugh. We ask them personal questions about how their day was or how their kids are and make them feel SPECIAL. We get to know them and make them feel like they belong.

A Trainer's role does not start when the class starts; they represent KX as soon as they step into the studio. Clients look up to them, as they are the professional in the room. They feel proud that clients have chosen THEIR class. Clients who favor Trainers don't do so by chance; they must like something specific about them, trust them. Our Trainers must make them feel a certain way for them to keep coming back.

2. EDUCATOR

Our Trainers play an important role in educating their clients. If the client is new to **KX**, a Trainer's job is to welcome them to the new style of fitness and the journey they are about to embark on. They must first ask questions about their fitness background, Pilates or reformer Pilates experience, and potential injuries to work through. Then they must educate them on the reformer, explaining what's involved, how it works, what to expect in a class, and why the **KX** method is different. First impressions last, and making our clients feel comfortable in this new and exciting environment is paramount.

3. BUDDY/CONNECTOR

Some clients' main focus when joining a new fitness studio may simply be to make friends or even to just be in a friendly environment. And if they don't feel like it's a friendly environment, they may never come back. This must start with the Trainer. They need to take the lead to be "professional friends" and connect with their clients on an individual level, look them in the eyes, remember their names, and ask question after question to get to know them and show interest. Once this is achieved, then the real influence and power comes from the Trainer connecting like-minded clients with each other. If a connection is made, and friendship blossoms, it's a recipe for retaining clients for life. To do this effectively though, first the Trainer must get to know their clients well so they can find commonalities they can then use to make these connections. It could be as simple as loving the same sporting team, their love for certain pets, their kids going to the same school, or the love of the best restaurants and cafes in town. Becoming a connector is one of the best traits a Trainer can have.

4. PUBLIC SPEAKER/PERFORMER

Our Trainers need to own the room. The KX class is there to let their personalities shine! They need to make KX classes their own. Dance, sing, crack jokes—it's all so important for connecting. Teaching a great class just isn't enough; they need to perform. Once again, Trainer individuality is not just encouraged at KX, but it is demanded. Some clients may not like each Trainer's style, which is totally OK, but others will love it. After all, KX is an EXPERIENCE that a client cannot go anywhere else to get. And that experience encapsulates everything.

5. TRAINER (it may seem obvious, but there is so much responsibility in their hands)

- REMEMBERING NAMES. KX Trainers are taught to remember names. Some people are naturals; others need help! But everyone feels special when they are greeted or spoken to by name. I remember I used to draw rectangles on a sheet of paper each class to represent a reformer and write each client's name on it for reference. Repetition works and after a while, it sticks. It doesn't matter how many times you ask someone their name; it's still better than forgetting it and never referring to them by it!

- APPROPRIATE TOUCH. Something that is so important. Physical connection is crucial, even if it is a light touch on the shoulder to say hello. Our Trainers should be touching at least HALF of their clients every exercise, not only to correct postural alignment, but to make them feel that their personal attention is solely on that client—and no one else—for that split second. Our Trainers are even taught to touch those who are doing the exercise perfectly, as those 3–5 seconds make it a PERSONAL experience.

- ASSIST EVERY STRETCH. Again, this is where touch continues for our Trainers. Every stretch our clients perform, our Trainers are assisting at least half of the class.

- VOICE. Our Trainers are taught to use their voice. They can be loud. They can be quiet. They can drag an exercise on longer to be cheeky and tease the client with muscle fatigue before they stop! We allow their personality to shine through their voice. They learn to use their voice to display their PASSION.

- REFRESH. They change up their class plans and sequences on a regular basis to make the class new, dynamic, fluid and fun. Some of our clients come most days of the week, every week!

So, continuing to change in a way that provides new challenges is key. Our Trainers are also our clients; they love KX just as much as they love to teach it, and informal play and trial and error leads to new exercises. Even after twelve years and with the imagination we allow in our sessions, we still see amazing new exercises being created. It really blows my mind.

- EQUALITY. Although every client is different, has a different fitness background, and has different strengths and weaknesses, our Trainers include everyone. Of course, we have our select Beginner, Intermediate and Advanced classes to specify the workout type, but, even in those broad categories, we teach Trainers to give different spring options to progress and regress each exercise so it can be tailored to the individual.

- FINISH ON A HIGH. So important, no different than building a house. The last five percent is the most important to make the entire class come together. They bring the class to an end with a sequence of stretching, breathing techniques, or an exercise finisher to really feel the burn before the class is over. They are grateful to each and every client for participating and coming to their class.

6. EXPERT

When the class is finished, our Trainers' work continues. They ask the clients if they have any questions about the class, how they are feeling, or go into more specific details on certain stretches or moves clients may want to know more about. And, most importantly, they congratulate. KX classes are tough! Feedback is also asked for, as we are always wanting to improve. It's also a great time to discuss what class levels are suitable for what clients moving forward. After a fifty min class, the Trainer now knows your body and how it moves, so if they don't come forth with the information, just ask!

KX TRAINER TESTIMONIALS

What is it You Love About Pilates/KX?

"I love how accessible it is to every 'body.' It's empowering for people to see how strong their bodies can be even with an injury and even without harsh impact style workouts."

—Hannah, KX Hampton

"First and foremost, the workout! There really is no other fitness regime that can sculpt and tone the body in fifty minutes like a KX class does. The vibe at KX Pilates is so unique. All of us teachers have built really great relationships with our clients, and seeing their growth and progress over time is really special!"

—Dani, KX Miami

"I love Pilates as it is a unique workout that leaves your body feeling both lengthened and strengthened! I like that it is a safe way to challenge your muscles, in that you can attempt advanced moves that challenge stability, coordination, and strength without putting excessive stress/strain on the joints. But my favorite thing about KX is the community that surrounds it. I get to go work out amongst amazing clients that continually inspire me and, most importantly, make me laugh and have a good time."

—Emma, KX Port Melbourne

Why Do You Love Teaching?

"I love helping people to feel good about themselves. If they walk in the door in a poor state of mind, I hope they walk out feeling motivated, energetic, and ready to tackle life!"

—Tallulah, KX Williamstown

"I love teaching because I love being able to support clients on their fitness journeys no matter what stage they're at. I love being able to share my passion for movement in such a fun, upbeat environment. Being able to educate and encourage people to be active and how

their bodies move in space is such a special thing, and I feel so lucky to do it as my job!"

—Shahnae, KX Yarraville

"I enjoy helping clients on their journey, from starting out in their first class to the weeks and months watching them progress and become stronger. First, I see major changes in their mindset, which then results in changes to their bodies. This in turn gives them better results, which in full circle is a gift they give themselves. I enjoy seeing change, and I enjoy challenging people to get the best out of themselves."

—Andrew, KX Berwick

"Teaching KX and working alongside our clients is extremely rewarding! It's incredibly gratifying to see clients improve over time and see them notice the changes and the abilities within themselves."

—Eva, KX Williamstown

KX REBRAND NEARS COMPLETION

The rebrand was nearly complete. Daz delivered the finishing touches, including design motifs, brand fonts, style guides, and studio design templates. Impressed was an understatement. I was more confident than ever that KX had been transformed and now had the professionalism needed to go forth and conquer.

The rebrand had me pumped. What else could I do with KX? They say that it's common for entrepreneurial minds to always look for the next big shiny thing to focus on and quickly get bored with the "now." This definitely happened to me. You could say that my ambition started to get the better of me. Although KX Pilates was going well, I found myself feeling stale and wondering what was next. I wanted KX to be more than

> What if KX could be more than just a Pilates brand? What if it were a fitness movement?

just a top Pilates brand in Australia, and the idea of expanding excited the hell out of me. Really, I wanted KX to be the Virgin of the fitness world. At the time, I might have likened my ambition to that of the great Richard Branson. His books definitely inspired me!

I started to visualize how we could get the KX experience and all we had to offer to more fitness enthusiasts. I wanted more people to live the KX way of life. When KX is a part of your everyday existence, life is better!

LESSONS LEARNED

1. Find the ability to separate your personal feelings from your business and look at it from a business perspective. This is where external advisors are invaluable, as they may see things in your blind spot. Try to remove emotion from your decisions—this is a lot easier said than done!

2. A brand is a feeling—take the time to create and build it. What is your brand? Do customers feel a certain way when they walk into your workplace, visit your website, or contact an employee? How can you influence this?

3. Find something new in what you are already doing. A rebrand/refresh can breathe life back into your business. Or, in our case, it made KX put its professional pants on.

"There is no innovation and creativity without failure. Period."

—Brené Brown

Chapter 6

NOT FAILURE. EXPENSIVE LESSONS.

After three years of growing KX Pilates, my ambition to do more was overwhelming.

I saw KX as more than Pilates. I could see multiple brands dominating multiple fitness disciplines, and I was constantly researching fitness brands online and going to the US on reconnaissance missions. I observed which fitness styles were gaining popularity and imagined them in Australia under the KX brand. It wasn't long until I risked it all again.

I thought I could innovate outside the core of KX Pilates and still deliver the same personalized experience with other fitness options, but this approach did not work well. Let's just say that my aspirations resulted in a lot of lessons.

EXPANDING BEYOND PILATES

KX Pilates

Founded in 2010–present
www.kxpilates.com.au
@kxpilates

I credit KX's start-up success to my passion, determination, dedication, and willingness to succeed no matter the cost. Timing played a major factor, but my support network was also crucial. I did what I had to in order to learn what I didn't know. Although I was massively pushed out of my comfort zone, I persisted and when the time came—and thank God it did—it was then about bringing the right people on board to help make my dream a reality. Those people then became the reason for KX's success. It became *our* brand, and we did it together.

KX Retreats

Founded in 2012—paused in 2020
due to COVID
www.kxretreats.com.au
@kxretreats

After a couple years of growing KX Pilates, with two studios to our name, an old schoolmate came to me with the idea of starting fitness retreats in Bali. His main business at the time was in blinds and awnings, so he made most of his money in the summer months, with winter being incredibly slow. This downtime saw him head overseas on surfing trips, and it was on these trips that he realized there was a market: a fitness retreat space that KX would fit right into. He had the idea and the business drive, and I had the brand, Trainers, and clientele pull it off.

Kubu Private Beach, Ayana Resort, Bali, Indonesia

At that time, there were ladies-only surf and yoga retreats in the hustle and bustle of Seminyak or more intense cheap and cheerful boot-camp-style fitness retreats in the mountains. With his idea, the KX brand, my reach to potential clients, and my passion for travel, it was a no-brainer to give it a shot.

We wanted to separate ourselves from the perfect clean eating style that came with other retreats and move away from the "fat camp" attitude and strict training scenario that came with others. We would run five different training sessions per day, and all were optional. If you wanted a glass of wine over dinner, that was completely fine. We looked at it more like a fitness holiday where like-minded clients could come and relax, get fit, enjoy themselves, and, most of all, have fun.

In our first year, we only ran two retreats. We started to gain momentum in our second year and ran four, but something just didn't feel right. Our business relationship was taxing. We disagreed a lot about the company's direction, and it started to impact my life negatively. We went in fifty-fifty, which meant no one had an overarching say or total control, and we found ourselves arguing over minor details. Because we were both control freaks, we clashed constantly. We were also hitting a target market that differed from our average KX clientele. Our website and flyers had 18–25-year-old girls with perfect bikini bodies, and I was starting to hear from Trainers and clients that our marketing direction was beginning to intimidate our clientele instead of motivating them to come along. We were also burning through cash and not making anything.

We would do deals for certain clients or friends behind closed doors to boost retreat numbers, but then they'd boast to the full-fee-paying guests on the retreat. Understandably, they left feeling ripped off. There were also free retreats given to influencers and celebrities to market the business on their social media. I wasn't comfortable with the path we were taking.

Six retreats and eighteen months later, I ended our partnership—quite amicably, I might add. The business he wanted and the path I imagined for KX were just two different things. He completely understood where I was coming from and, soon after, launched his own Active Escapes company, which has done very well. The concept, however, just didn't align with the vision I had for KX.

After the split, I agreed not to run a retreat for two years. In 2015, we relaunched KX Retreats, which, before COVID, ran up to four events per year. It's a fantastic lifestyle business that has many benefits. Firstly, it gave us an avenue to recognize our most valuable and loyal Trainers by making them guest Trainers on retreat, an incredible opportunity for them and their clients. Secondly, it strengthened the KX brand. I love that we've created something outside of our KX studios where clients can connect, relax, rejuvenate, take a holiday, and come back feeling amazing.

It's incredible how many powerful connections you can make with people when you share a retreat with them for seven days.

KX Retreats also provided heavy discounts for Franchise Partners and Trainers. On top of that, Franchise Partners received referral fees when their studio clients attended, and, as of 2019, all profits from KX Retreats went back into the marketing fund to improve the KX brand as a whole. A win-win.

We also partnered with some amazing people. Our resort accommodation was on the quiet east coast of Bali, with excellent fitness and hotel facilities, not to mention outstanding food. For variety, each retreat had a different guest trainer, and it was one of the best weeks of the year for many clients. Repeat clientele is also something we saw more of as the retreats continued.

KX Retreats remains on pause while we focus on getting KX Pilates back and firing on all cylinders, both nationally and internationally post-COVID.

KX Barre

Founded in 2013, absorbed into KX Pilates in 2017, ended in 2019

The ballet barre method had massive traction in the US and UK, and one of our top Trainers, Rachael Fraser, was an English lass who'd trained in this method in her home country. Rachael, an ex-dancer, was working for both KX and a barre studio in Melbourne's CBD.

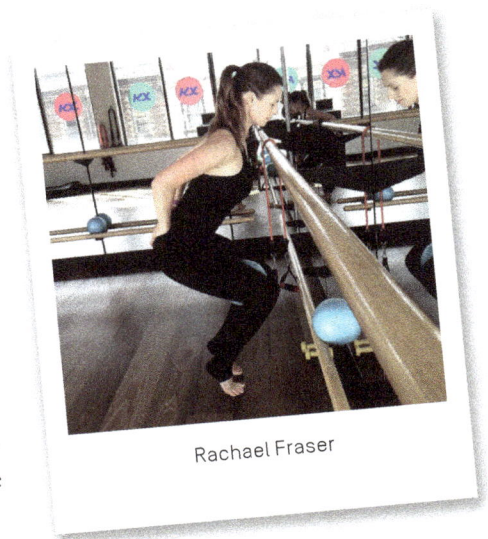

Rachael Fraser

Xtend Barre, an American franchise, had a dancer-orientated offering that appealed to professional and ex-professional dancers who wanted to stay fit. However, the feedback I kept hearing suggested that unless you were a dancer and knew the basics, attending classes was intimidating. Barre Body, a former Melbourne-founded company, also opened a studio that instead offered a barre-yoga fusion, mixing elements of the two styles and seeing fast success.

I saw a gap in the market where KX could fit. Firstly, we could appeal to clients who were new to the ballet barre world and offer technique-focused beginner classes. Secondly, we could also provide a more high-performance Pilates-barre mix in line with KX Pilates. Another point of difference would be our equipment. A regular barre class used just one ballet barre at waist height but if we were going to bring in a more Pilates-focused method, I thought that having a second ballet barre at knee height—a similar height to where a foot bar is on the reformer—where more Pilates moves could be performed would be a differential idea.

And so, in 2013, KX Barre was born.

Credit here must go to the dedication and effort that Rachael put in to create KX Barre. Already one of our top KX Pilates instructors, Rachael spent hours perfecting the KX Barre Academy. Unfortunately, KX Barre just ended up being KX Pilates' poor cousin. It was never our primary focus. I was never passionate enough about it to have that "do anything and everything to make it succeed no matter the cost" attitude, as I was still heavily focused on growing KX Pilates. As the saying goes, "Where focus goes, energy flows." We ended up folding barre back into KX Pilates as an additional class type in 2017.

In my view, barre was more of a short-lived fad than a genuine trend in the Australian fitness industry. As a result, we shut down the offering entirely in 2019. It was probably a blessing in disguise to get out when we did—an expensive but worthwhile lesson!

KX Yoga
Founded in 2013, sold, and rebranded in 2016
@hereyoga

KX Yoga reception, 2013

Life is all about timing. As I was getting KX Barre up and running, a space became available next to my KX Pilates Malvern studio. With a small tip-off from my landlord stating that another fitness brand may be moving in, I was quick to snap up the space and prepare for the launch of KX Yoga.

I had been a client of Hot Yoga Studios in Melbourne for some time and found great benefit in adding a hot Vinyasa flow to my weekly training regime. It was also an excellent opportunity to catch up with old friends. Although I never got into yoga's mindfulness and meditation, I saw significant benefits from a flexibility, strength, and balance standpoint. On top of that, it was nice to escape Melbourne's cold winters in warm yoga studios.

I tried Bikram yoga a few times and was not a fan at all. But Hot Yoga Studios seemed to target people like me who despised Bikram. It offered beautifully designed studios, a friendly feel, and each class was different from the previous one, unlike Bikram, which has the same sequence in every session. Most classes on the schedule ran to sixty minutes, as opposed to Bikram's ninety minutes, which I believed was perfect.

I was constantly in bustling studios and never felt that I was ever doing it right. One

As a yoga client and owner of an experience-based business, I was never satisfied with the experience all around and thought that it could be done better.

day, after the class, the teacher even asked me what was wrong with my shoulder, as she had noticed I was leaning to one side during the downward dog. I was annoyed because there was nothing wrong with my shoulder. In reality, I was just doing the pose wrong, and my body awareness in that position sucked. But she hadn't corrected me during class. There were way too many people jammed in the room, and the trainers weren't instructed to help us individually. Instead, they were taught to teach the masses and had no time to give individual attention or correct poor technique. That was the final straw for me, and I had to do something to put the KX mark on the yoga industry.

I reached out to Jolene Galea. She had been one of the part-time KX bookkeepers for a few years and was looking to drop off her accounting work to follow her passion and teach yoga full-time. She mentioned the idea of an assistant teacher, which she'd seen in some studios. This would allow beginner instructors to assist an experienced teacher for free to gain experience in a teaching environment and learn from a more experienced leader. Their job would be to assist and correct students in poses and help introduce new clients to the world of yoga. But there were two downsides. Firstly, being amateur teachers, they lacked experience, and we couldn't guarantee they'd be any good. Secondly, because they were not being paid for the class, it would be difficult to hold them accountable to even show up. Then I saw KX Yoga's main point of difference. We would become the first fully-assisted yoga studio in Melbourne, and Jolene would be the headteacher and manager.

The idea was solid. We would have two teachers in each class, one being the headteacher taking the class and the other directly assisting students by either correcting their poses, helping with body awareness and correct positioning, or pushing them deeper into advanced practice. What an experience!

It was a brilliant concept. Clients loved it, and we were definitely doing something different in the yoga industry at the time. The studio became busy quickly, but that busyness in the studio didn't translate to a successful business. Expenses far outweighed the income generated. To match the boutique experience at KX Pilates at the time, we offered sweat towels and water. In the beginning, students would use not just one towel each but up to six to cover their mat, so the laundry expenses shot up six times compared to a standard KX Pilates studio. They also used the small sweat towels to dry themselves after a shower! And, of course, offering water stopped any purchases from the fridge.

But even after we got rid of the towels, there were three main reasons why KX Yoga was another expensive lesson:

1. The additional expenses that came by paying the adjuster teacher meant that teacher costs were three times the price of a KX Pilates class.

2. We ran workshops but never ran teacher training. It is now known that teacher training is close to fifty percent of revenue for most yoga studios. Even students who don't want to be teachers often want to learn and expand on their yoga journey, so they're an easy sell when they are already connected to your studio and teachers.

3. Yoga is for the masses. This was probably the biggest eye-opener for me and just showed how stuck I was in the boutique fitness world of Pilates, where a single class is $30, and clients never hesitated when paying for their next session or block pack.

When I was doing yoga before starting this business, I looked around. I calculated how many people were in the class, estimating the rent and outgoings to arrive at the average cost per session. I was off by a lot! With yoga bringing in all socioeconomic walks of life, it attracts many who are chasing the cheapest deals possible. They will either hold out until a sale or just roam from studio to studio doing their intro packs. With the growing number of yoga studios in Melbourne, most offering the same intro pack—fourteen days unlimited for $30—it's a very cheap way to participate. Due to the additional expenses we had that others didn't, we hurt the most.

Luckily for me, an amazing human by the name of Sarah and her husband at the time, Ian, came to me wanting to get involved. Both yogis wanted their own studio but didn't want to start from scratch. I initially sold a majority stake in the business to them but after twelve months, when my focus went back one hundred percent to KX Pilates, I gave my minority share to them in 2016 so they could rebrand and go their own way. They were much better operators, passionate about yoga, and, to this day, Here Yoga is a very successful business.

Jolene's love of Yoga soon switched to a love of Pilates. She trained in KX and eventually opened multiple KX studios in Sydney with her now-husband, Chris. Another example of timing and relationships working in sync together!

KX Cycle
Co-founded in 2015, rebranded as
United Ride in 2017, sold in 2019
@unitedride

Having traveled to the US, I was familiar with Soul Cycle and was a huge fan. Everything about the business impressed me, from the people, workout, branding, and energy when you walked through the doors to the buzzing atmosphere of the classes. When Eli, my first follower and business partner in the KX Pilates Richmond studio, and her friend Ali came to me with the proposal of opening a cycle studio modeling the Soul Cycle concept, I was excited for the opportunity to do something like it in Australia and jumped at the chance to be involved.

In 2015, we cofounded **KX Cycle**. It was a side project for me and quite an advantageous deal. I would put up no capital for a minority stake in the business, and they could operate under the **KX** banner to piggyback off our marketing, website, and brand. If successful, it would be an easy sell into the existing network of **KX Franchise Partners** as a bolt-on cardio offering. Unfortunately, we didn't get past first gear. Initial capital expenditure blew out, and the build costs were extravagant, almost double that of a standard **KX Pilates** studio. The business didn't fail, but, when I was involved, it just never succeeded. We never had to tip any additional capital into it, and it paid for its own operation for the first two years.

United Ride. Richmond (VIC)
www.unitedride.com.au

When the time came to take back the **KX** brand, I offered them the same deal as **KX Yoga**, but they were understandably reluctant to pump more money into the business until it started showing a return. Instead, I spent $30,000, rebranded **KX Cycle** to United Ride in 2017, and relaunched the new brand, hoping it could "ride on its own two wheels." However, we still saw no real return.

Eventually, we all agreed that the people "riding" at the top needed to change, so Ali and I sold our share in 2019 to pave the way for a new owner to try her luck. It always seemed like a successful business; we had many loyal clients who loved our concept. However, in Australia, spin classes at gyms are extremely popular, and, compared to the price of one United Ride class, you could have a week of unlimited spin classes. But fingers crossed that the new blood in the business can make it into the success we always wanted.

KX Life
Founded in 2015, closed in 2016, returned via the KX App in 2020 due to COVID-19

Another chapter in the KX history books is KX Life. We founded in 2015, closed in 2016, and reopened in 2020 when COVID forced us out of the studios. It taught me a precious lesson: always make sure you are in control.

Cast your mind back to 2015 when every Instagrammer with a following started doing their own at-home workouts and eating plans. Most had no qualifications in fitness or nutrition, but this didn't seem to matter to their audience. We were approached by an online wellness company with a complete training, nutrition, and mindfulness platform that we reskinned and called KX Life. Membership was $50/month, which gave subscribers full access to articles, blogs, eating plans, recipes, and at-home "anywhere, anytime" bodyweight training programs.

In theory, the offering was pretty impressive, and it complemented what KX Pilates had to offer. However, the cost of the platform was huge, as the company behind it was trying to recoup their exorbitant build costs. Uptake was reasonably good for the thirteen studios we had at that time, but the expenses far outweighed the benefits. After twelve months in the red, we went back to renegotiate prices, but they canceled the contract. Instead of working through a reputable fitness brand like KX, the company had decided to put all its resources into celebrity fitness faces who could sell their platform. We should have seen it coming via the Instagram wave; people follow people, not brands. So, we wrapped up.

Due to our pivot to online classes in 2020 due to COVID-19, KX Life returned in all its glory, this time under our control. More explained in the COVID-19 chapter.

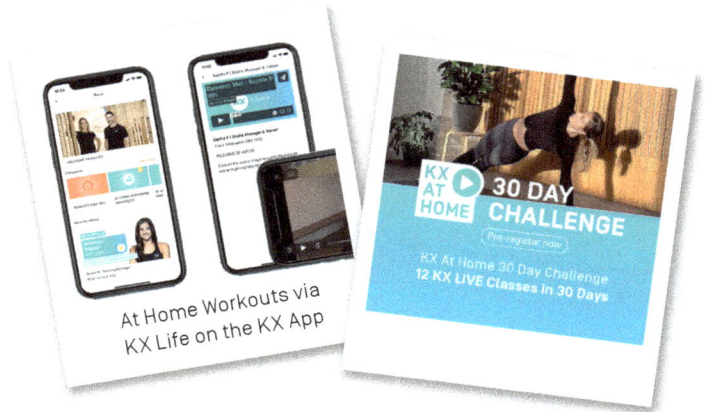

At Home Workouts via
KX Life on the KX App

LESSONS LEARNED

1. Don't start anything unless you can dedicate all the time needed to make it successful, or chances are you've already failed.

2. Be careful of partnerships and enter them with caution. It's easy to get excited about going into business with someone else, and it has many advantages. But if things were to go wrong, what would happen to the relationship? If you do go down that path, always have shareholder agreements or formal contracts in place.

3. Always do your research. Test the business idea—never assume. Assumptions can turn into expensive lessons. Testing is a cheap way to know you're wrong before you invest thousands.

"Life is change.
Growth is optional.
Choose wisely."

—Einstein

Chapter 7

IF NOTHING CHANGES, THEN NOTHING CHANGES

My goal for KX was never to be ordinary. Just as I wanted more for my life, I wanted KX to grow, develop and move forward. More than anything, I wanted KX to lead the boutique fitness industry and to leave competitors in our wake.

An experienced franchisor once told me:

> *"When implementing or attempting to implement change in a franchise network, the more you can work the scenario to make the franchisees believe that the idea and the decision for change are theirs, and you as franchisor are just there to execute it for them, the more likely that change will be adopted and succeed."*

Great advice, but much easier said than done! Change is hard to implement, but it's especially hard across a franchise.

With these words in mind, in 2016, KX embarked on a year of change.

1. The Marketing Fund

Our National Marketing Fund was not collecting enough money to drive the activities and results we needed. The fund, in general, is somewhat of a controversial topic. Within the franchise, ongoing royalties are easily justified as the cost of having "KX Pilates" on your door and getting access to all the necessary systems and support. However, money spent on marketing is constantly questioned because the franchisor spends it at their discretion—within the marketing guidelines in the Franchise Code of Conduct, of course. The marketing team, which consisted of Andi for over five years, also draws their salary from the Marketing Fund. Andi was unquestionably underpaid for her expertise and experience. But, because she was my partner, it was an easy target for controversy.

The Marketing Fund was always set at two percent of revenue, but we quickly realized that it did not equate to a lot based on the low revenues per studio. On July 1, 2016, we doubled the marketing fund to four percent of revenue for all new Partners that joined the franchise. Company-owned studios followed suit immediately to set the standard and comply with the franchise code.

Now we had the fun part of communicating the changes to three stakeholder groups.

a. New Franchise Partners

This was the easiest to communicate. The four percent contribution to the marketing fund would be in place for all future studios and potential Franchise Partners—some we hadn't even met yet!

b. Prospective Franchise Partners

Potential Franchise Partners in the pipeline were informed that the marketing fund contribution would double from the figure initially discussed. With rational thinking and positioning, this was also well received.

c. Existing Franchise Partners

This was a tough sell. At that time, the current Franchise Partners in the network were on their first of two five-year terms, totaling a ten-year agreement. Due to the franchise agreement they had already signed, we couldn't immediately make changes to their marketing fund contribution overnight.

We could have just waited until their initial terms were up before we implemented the changes, but that wouldn't have helped us solve the immediate need for more marketing dollars.

So, we put forward two options:

Option 1: They would agree to change to three percent from July 1 until the conclusion of their initial term. If they opted for this, we would continue to honor three percent into their second term.

Option 2: They remained at two percent for the rest of their term and would jump to four percent for their second.

We explained that choosing Option 1 would save them anywhere between $10,000–$30,000 throughout their ten-year agreements. While Option 2 would have put more money into the marketing fund over the long run, we felt that encouraging Franchise Partners to choose Option 1 would fund the acceleration it needed to put the company in a stronger marketing position earlier compared to Option 2.

Most Franchise Partners chose Option 1, and we considered it a success. But there were a handful who chose Option 2. These were the "negative players" at the time. Looking back, I realize they weren't interested in a compromise that would benefit them for the second term of their agreement because they weren't planning to be around for it. In the years that followed, the majority of those who chose Option 2 exited KX.

2. Facebook Permissions

Facebook has always been an essential channel in our marketing strategy.

You might remember that in 2016, Facebook changed its permissions structure literally overnight. It introduced a two-tier access system with one master access tier to control everything, and one manager access tier that could do everything the master could, other than add more admins.

This might sound like a small change, but for KX and our Franchise Partner network that relies on Facebook as a primary communications channel, it was a very big deal! I'll explain why. As the franchisor, due to obvious IP protection rights, we own everything to do with the business: databases, permissions, and email and social media accounts. Not only are these things owned by us for the reasons stated above, but if the Franchise Partner wishes to sell, apart from the person or entity running the franchise, everything stays in one place. When you pay your franchise fee and ongoing royalties, you get the license to operate all of the above.

Now, in the early stages of the business, we gave master access for

Facebook accounts to both Franchise Partner and franchisor. These accounts need to link to an individual, so Andi, as Head of Marketing at the time, was each page's head office representative. As soon as Andi received news of the changes from Facebook, she was also notified that one studio had removed her from all permissions on its Facebook page! This meant that we were completely locked out of that particular studio's page.

Andi and I discussed the implications of this happening at a larger scale across the business, and we acted quickly. We took over master access of the entire network and gave each owner-manager access. We then contacted the network to explain what we had done. While ninety percent of the network were completely understanding, a handful of studios felt betrayed, as if we had stolen something from them. Some even demanded the thousands of dollars they had put into Facebook advertising to be paid back to them. The crazy thing is, they already knew we owned all the social media accounts, as this was agreed prior and stated upfront in their Franchise Agreements.

This experience taught us a lot about timely and effective communication versus reacting.

In franchising, the brand comes first over any individual's opinion. This experience highlighted that it wasn't a Facebook permission issue but a communication, relationships, and trust issue. Our Franchise Partners felt that we didn't trust them because we acted before we discussed it with them. It's a shame that we had to act and change the entire network without their buy-in because of the few people who proved themselves untrustworthy.

While it was the right choice to protect the KX brand and not act on the feelings of a few Franchise Partners, as a founder, you have to take the time to set expectations from the outset and ensure that everyone involved understands.

3. Sham Contracting

The most significant change we implemented in 2016 landed us in court.

The accepted standard in the Australian boutique fitness industry is for a trainer to sign an Independent Contractors Agreement (ICA) where the trainer is a subcontractor, has their own personal or company ABN, and invoices the business for their time. This method benefits employers because they do not have to pay WorkCover, superannuation, sick, personal, or annual leave and can basically fire the trainer on the spot with no repercussions. With this method, there is also less bookkeeping involved, as the employer does not have to deduct tax from the trainer's pay, which they would have to do with an employee.

It is also widely accepted by trainers who work for multiple studios or businesses, as they are not taxed at a higher rate for having additional jobs. They can also claim logoed training wear, motor vehicle expenses, and anything else their accountant advises is a work-related expense. On an ICA, by law, the trainer can also quit work without giving any notice.

Although this may be a symbiotic relationship and common in the fitness industry, it doesn't make it legal or morally right. In fact, it's known in the employment world as "sham contracting." Business.gov.au defines it as, "When an employer attempts to disguise an employment relationship as a contractor relationship. They may do this to avoid certain taxes and their responsibility for employee entitlements like minimum wages, super-annuation, leave."[6]

In my early days as a PT, sham contracting was prominent. When it came to KX, we needed to know if we were doing the right thing by our Trainers.

In 2015, we had obtained legal advice, which suggested that some of our Trainers could be employees. But it still wasn't one hundred percent clear unless we were challenged on a case-by-case basis. After discussions with the small number of Franchise Partners that we had at the time, we agreed to continue to pay our Trainers as contractors but mitigate our risks by paying WorkCover and superannuation. This meant we were paying them the benefits that mattered. It would also mean Trainers could remain free to work where they wished without being penalized—a win-win for everyone.

It was about this time that the 7-Eleven underpayment scandal hit the news, which prompted the Federal Senate Inquiry into Franchising. Two years later, franchisor-Franchise Partner joint liability laws passed, which meant that if a Franchise Partner broke employment laws in any way, the franchisor was equally responsible.

During this time, KX had opened eighteen studios in eighteen months, and, with these new laws in place, we reviewed our employment contracts again and decided all of our trainers would now need to fall under employment law and become employees of each studio they worked for. We drew up draft contracts and communicated the changes to the entire network. Although this was expensive and Trainers would change what they'd been doing for most of their careers, we were doing the right thing.

If we wanted to be leaders in the Australian fitness industry, we had to be leaders in every way, even if it cost us to do so. Unfortunately, not every Franchise Partner agreed. Due to confidentiality, I cannot disclose the details, but let's just say there was a complete communication breakdown, lawyers got involved, and we went to court.

The experience taught me that you need to try to resolve any conflict without lawyers. Effective communication is critical, which is why mediation is so effective in the franchise world both for communication, rectification, and cost-effectiveness. If you end up in court, the only people who win are the lawyers. With time passing and old wounds healed, all involved have made amends, and a positive relationship continues.

We all learned an incredible amount about how NOT to conduct ourselves.

4. Stepping Back as CEO

Being the CEO of a franchise is demanding but also incredibly rewarding. There are so many positives to growing a franchise business—I would jump out of bed every day, obsessively focused on creating something amazing. I lived for the look on Franchise Partners' faces when they opened their studio doors for the very first time. The close-knit relationships you forge at the beginning are powerful but the reality is, the bigger you grow, the harder it is to sustain the same personal connection with the network, and you inevitably put others in your place to do so.

I think I was an *okay* boss.

I was never a good manager, never gave enough personal praise to people, and was terrible at setting KPIs and following them up. But I made work fun by adopting the forty-nine percent friend, fifty-one percent boss mentality. KX was a lifestyle brand, and people came to work at our head-quarters because they loved the brand and loved the people.

As the team grew, however, my lack of management experience became obvious. Some staff abused the free rein I gave them, and others simply refused to work a minute longer than they had to. I was also terrible at cracking the whip. Not because I feared confrontation—I liked that a little too much—but because I couldn't empathize. I came across as harsh and unfair. After the court case and a few other issues within the network, I realized that I needed help running the company.

I spent a lot of time reading business books and tapping into my growing network of mentors. Jim Collins' classic line says that to grow your business, you have to put the right people in the right seats on the bus.[7] I had been driving that metaphorical bus for a while, and being the CEO and founder is the most taxing job I have ever had.

Was I the right person to take KX to the next level? My heart and my head were telling me that I was not.

At about the time we reached thirty studios, I knew something had to change. The faster we grew, the more problems we saw, which led to sleepless nights and my waning interest in the top job.

This coincided with me becoming a father to Archer, born in late 2015, who made me realize what's truly important in life. Everything I had been getting caught up with at work meant nothing. I no longer wanted to be the best CEO of my company—my goal had changed to being the best father I could be.

I dropped off Mondays from work to spend time with Archer, and he became our little KX mascot. We made him a KX top—which became an icon in years to come—with "Trainer in the making" on it, and he would join us at studio openings, events, and birthdays. Everyone loved him. Just seventeen months later, his sister Ava arrived, and life became a little more challenging. Andi and I realized we couldn't both give the business our full-time support, which was even more reason to step aside.

At the time, I had a business advisor with whom I'd worked for about eighteen months. Coincidentally, his new business venture did not go as planned, and he had some free time. He already knew the ins and outs of KX and had a lot of relevant experience: 24/7 gym franchising, taking a brand to an Asian market, strong with numbers, strategy, and analytics. Coupled with the fact we already had a good working relationship, he seemed like a good fit. His strengths were the opposite of mine, and I thought we would make a good team. I appointed him Chief Operating Officer (COO) and agreed that in twelve months, if all went well, he would be the first non-founding CEO of KX Pilates.

Nine months later, we called it quits. We amicably agreed that he wasn't the right fit for KX.

I learned a lot during this time.

a. Culture is king

"Change the leader, change the team" is a common saying, but it's something else to experience in real life. He moved away from a horizontal structure at headquarters to more hierarchical management. When you have been treating people equally since the beginning, it's pretty hard for them to swallow hierarchy. Couple that with personality clashes, and it was only a matter of six months before half of the HQ team had moved on.

Some Franchise Partners were also unhappy and voiced their opinions regularly. They were behind the new direction and strategy, but they didn't feel as if they were valued anymore. This negative effect on the KX culture taught me just how important culture is. Our COO's departure also revealed to me how quickly it could come back.

b. Think big(ger)

Before my advisor came on board as COO, our goal was 150 studios in Australia, an achievable target. After a trip with him to the International Franchise Conference in Phoenix in 2018, that goal moved to 500 studios globally. That same year we sold our first International Regional Master Franchise and witnessed our first international studio open in Jakarta, Indonesia.

He opened my eyes to how far we could take the KX brand beyond Australia and to the world.

c. Innovate within

I always asked: what else can we bolt on to KX to create more revenue for the business? We renegotiated rebates and tightened contracts with suppliers. We brought new suppliers on board. Lax expenses were reined in or cut out completely. As cliche as it might sound—always think outside the box.

5. Bridging the Gap

I first met Selina Bridge in March 2016.

Andi had worked with Selina at BMW in the early noughties when she was in marketing and events. We'd initiated the meeting because, at the time, our son Archer was just four months old, and Andi needed help heading up the marketing department so she could step back.

The discussion did not progress as we expected.

We quickly learned that Selina had been appointed General Manager of the female fitness franchise Curves in Australia and New Zealand (Australasia). She had worked her way up from Head of Marketing. Understandably, she wasn't interested in going back to a marketing role.

There was something about Selina that resonated with us both that day. She is intelligent, respectful, kind, fit, healthy, and very much on-brand with KX. She talked about her loyalty to her Curves franchisees, how much she loved franchise partner relationships, and the challenges that came with them. I knew it would not be the last time we met.

Over the next few years, Selina and I caught up for coffee every few months and discussed franchising, people, relationships, business, the balancing act of being a working parent, and running a franchise. We had a lot in common, except one thing: KX was growing, and Curves was on the decline. Our conversations would end with me asking her how she was going at Curves and if she was happy. Each time she was just as passionate as the last. There was something about sticking together as a network at a time of closures and terminations that I believe made her network stronger, and no doubt many stayed on or re-signed for another term because of her leadership.

In 2017, I reached out to Selina with an offer to become our COO, which she declined. For one, I could not afford her. Curves was private equity-backed, paid exceptionally well, and had great bonuses in place. At the time, KX was only at thirty-five studios, whereas Curves had 140 franchises across Australasia. But I sensed Selina's frustration with her current situation.

Timing and persistence came into play.

Throughout 2018, when KX was trialing its first COO, Selina and I continued to catch up. As soon as our COO departed, Selina was one of the few people I quickly got in touch with. And although I sold the dream of KX and its future growth in both Australia and international markets, I knew that career progression was what would attract her to KX. I put the role of KX's first non-founding CEO on the table. With this came the freedom she had been looking for to run a company her way, with no one telling her what she could or couldn't do.

Previously, my approach was to hire someone in a COO role to sit under me for twelve months and then potentially progress to CEO, but with Selina, I just knew that she was the right person to take our company to the next stage of growth and beyond. Coming from a declining brand, she had a hell of a lot of experience with tough conversations and being in uncomfortable situations—and still, people stuck by her. Give her a growing brand, and the potential is endless.

Selina took the job of CEO and gained the love and respect of the network. Our family culture returned to KX, and she immediately commanded respect as a thought leader in the company.

Hiring Selina is one of KX's greatest success stories.

Selina Bridge;
KX's first non-founding CEO

LESSONS LEARNED

1. Take learnings out of every situation, especially the bad ones.

2. Don't be afraid to change things. Changing management is challenging but if you don't innovate, you will kill your business.

3. Pay attention to maintaining culture. If people around you don't share the same values and outlook, it is bound to become a problem. The faster you "cut the mooring line," the better.

"The goal is not to be perfect by the end. The goal is to be better by tomorrow."

—Simon Sinek

Chapter 8

EVOLUTION THROUGH INNOVATION

2017 Heralded a New Era: KX, the Lifestyle Brand.

After seven years of operation, we had matured as a brand and as a franchise. It was time to evolve the KX brand again.

The KX colors had always been bold, dark, and intense. This served us well in the beginning to position KX as a high-intensity fitness experience and away from the clinical and classical Pilates industry.

We renewed our focus around representing high-intensity fitness

while maintaining an elegant and sophisticated brand. We removed the dark color palette of **KX** that had started to feel too masculine and introduced brighter, fresher, crisper colors that felt more neutral.

We also decided to drop "Pilates" from the **KX** logo. Seven years after opening our first studio, we had a presence in every state in Australia, and we felt that "**KX**" was now strong enough to stand on its own.

Our tagline, "Define Yourself," remained, and it still is the heart of **KX**. But we did enhance our positioning.

DEFINE, DISCOVER and **DEVELOP** helped define shorter, sharper messaging.

DEFINE YOURSELF

DISCOVER YOUR POTENTIAL

DEVELOP YOUR STRENGTH

PROJECT SPARKLE: BRIGHT. CRISP. FRESH.

In 2018, every new KX studio opened with a fresh new look and feel. This was the third brand and studio innovation for KX, and it helped solidify us as innovators and leaders of the boutique fitness industry.

All existing studios were scheduled for a makeover.

Stage 1: External signage

All studios would swap out the old for new external signage by 2020 and take down any internal signage.

Stage 2: Studio design

Dark walls were painted white, and we changed the flooring and internal signage. We also added completely new timber standing desks at reception and matching custom seating and cabinetry throughout.

The studio makeover also included new assets, artwork, and photo-shoots. The lighter, brighter coloring looked fantastic.

Clients were super impressed. They loved the new look and feel. The positive comments and words of congratulations to our Franchise Partners lifted their spirits to an all-time high. There was a genuinely warm feeling in all the studios.

It's hard to apply change, especially when it costs money! The positive client feedback made all that hard work, time, and personal investment worth it.

New studio reception design

The Booking System

Our booking system has come a long way since the early days of booking classes in Microsoft Excel.

At that time, people called or emailed to reserve a spot in a class and paid over the phone or in studio. In 2011, we started using an American-based company called MindBodyOnline (MBO), which changed our business forever.

Clients could book, schedule, cancel, and pay online. The booking data we now had access to also gave us incredible sales and attendance insights that soon informed our marketing strategy. However, MBO was expensive and came with significant transaction fees that were a lot for our Franchise Partners. Additionally, MBO's software ran on outdated technology that made it slow, complicated, and expensive to make any custom changes. We needed a new, more flexible system. Finding one that allowed us to avoid the excessive costs associated with building our own system was challenging.

By pure coincidence, we were approached by a company called Hapana, a new startup at the time. They were servicing fitness businesses just like us who were frustrated with the inflexibility of "mainstream" booking systems. Their focus was to deliver an efficient, customizable system at a competitive price. Hapana was also a local company founded by a young Australian named Jarron Aizen—which we loved.

KX would be Hapana's first major franchise customer, so we were naturally a little nervous. But we put our trust in Jarron and his team from the get-go and built a great relationship. We white labeled and reskinned the Hapana system, and, in 2018, we migrated the entire company over to the now self-named "KX Booking System (or KXS)." Switching over to KXS, like any major technology change, came with its fair share of challenges. There were times when Franchise Partners were cursing the system change—and me!

I can honestly say that Jarron and his team fixed every problem that arose while at the same time sticking to the agreed timeline to develop custom features. The most critical custom feature was the **KX** passport option. Clients can now use sessions in any **KX** Pilates studio in Australia and, hopefully, one day, the world.

Staying comfortable for the wrong reasons is just not in KX Pilates' DNA.

Was it more of a risk to go with an unknown provider? Absolutely. It would have been easier to just stay with **MBO**. But we wanted to innovate to be the best, and taking calculated risks is a part of that.

KX Academy Goes Online

Amie and her team have constantly improved and adapted the course over the years to make the training we offer second to none. Taking the **KX** Academy online in 2018 was a huge move for us, and it streamlined the entire training process. It also transformed into a national program in 2020 when **COVID** hit, which made it even more amazing.

EQUIPMENT OVERHAUL

In a typical **KX** Pilates studio, each client performs their class on a reformer machine. Each client gets a set of dumbbells with weights ranging anywhere from 1–8 kilograms.

Up until 2019, studios used a variety of dumbbell brands. There was no consistency between studios, which could be confusing for clients attending more than one location.

Clients also used a Pilates ring—primarily for the warm-up—and a wooden pole used for standing exercises and balance. These had not changed since 2010 when we first opened.

This sparked the first question: "What could we add to our training repertoire to improve our workout?"

The wooden pole—an ugly-looking broomstick with rubber stoppers on the ends—was by far the most unprofessional piece of equipment on the studio floor. What if we replaced it with a weighted pole or poles that varied in weight to suit each client?

Then came the second question: "How would we maintain consistency throughout the network and improve the current accessories?"

This led to our own line of **KX**-branded accessories.

Testing Equipment

We started the search and a lengthy testing process.

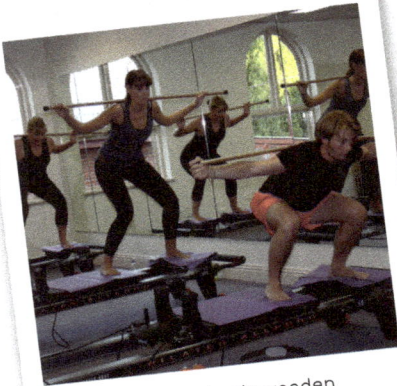

The original ugly wooden broomstick

INTRODUCING WEIGHTED POLES

Weighted Poles

Generic weighted poles on the market were ugly, too small, and poorly made. So began the process to customize a longer weighted pole, complete with KX branding. Each reformer machine now offered four poles ranging from 2–8 kilograms.

The launch of our weighted poles was a huge success. Clients and Trainers alike were excited about how these accessories added to their workout.

Dumbbells

Then came the introduction of our KX branded dumbbells. Each dumbbell was color-coded in KX tones to its weight, ranging from 1–8 kilograms. I loved these because it was an opportunity to showcase our brand pop-words on the sides:
PRESS—LIFT—PUSH—ELEVATE—
REACH—CONTROL

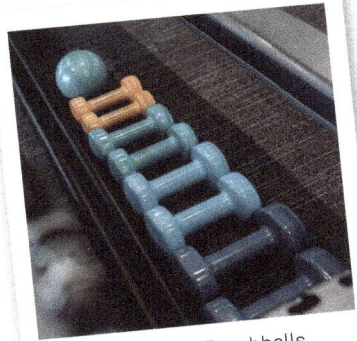
KX Custom Dumbbells

Pilates Ring and Toning Ball

Next was the Pilates ring. This was a custom collaboration with Balanced Body, which featured "KX" on the side of the knee pads.

Our toning ball was now in our KX "cool green" color with our tagline DEFINE YOURSELF printed in a neat circle. The entire range looked sharp, premium, and professional.

KX Toning Ball

The Reformer

The final and most crucial question on equipment innovation was about the heart of the KX workout: the reformer machine.

From the very beginning of KX, our classes were taught on the Balanced Body (BB) reformer machine: the Allegro (A1). The A1 was a workhorse, and no company in the world pushed their machines as hard as we did. According to BB, it was common knowledge that if there were an issue or fault with any part of the A1, KX Pilates' studios would find it first.

How Could we Improve the Reformer and Make it Our Own?

We were already customizing the A1 with a wider standing platform to accommodate the dynamic standing moves, such as squats and lunges, in the KX repertoire. These are exercises not often used in traditional Pilates. Although the A1 was a tough machine, it was still generic and had limitations. It had also been servicing the international Pilates market for over twenty years and was looking tired.

From the inception of KX Pilates in 2010, I had always wanted to create a machine specifically for the KX workout. I had seen people like Sebastien Lagree in the US develop machines like the "megaformer." I had watched his workout style move away from traditional Pilates and into his own fitness style, later named the "Lagree Fitness Method," but no one was really doing it in the Pilates industry.

KX Pilates, although highly intense and dynamic, was still Pilates, so it had to be performed on a Pilates reformer.

In 2013, Balanced Body released the Allegro 2 (A2), the first real innovation of the A1 for over a decade. It looked beautiful and stream-lined, with smooth lines and additional features that were of no actual use to the KX workout.

Due to a few early challenges that BB went through with the A2, we were advised *against* upgrading from the A1. The problem with that was

Balanced Body Allegro A1 Reformer

Balanced Body Allegro A2 Reformer

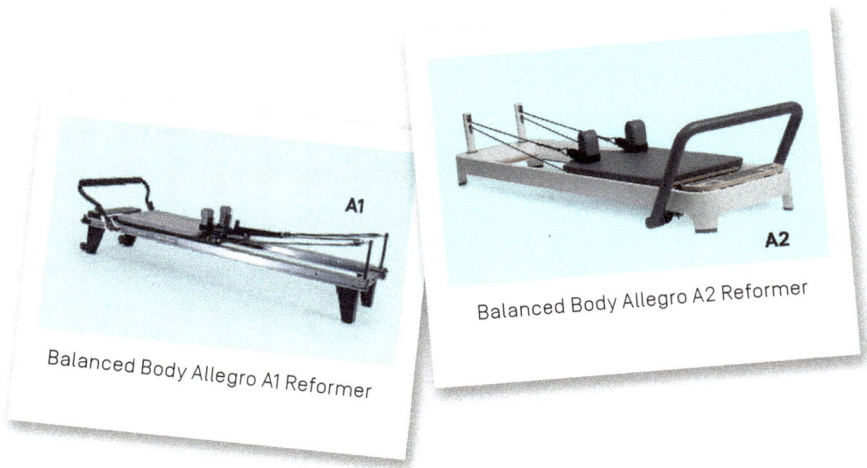

that competing Pilates studios did upgrade to the shiny new A2. And in the era of Instagram, the A2 was eye candy, and clients noticed! I wanted all the features of the A2, and then some, but it had to look way better.

Creating a custom machine is much easier said than done. Five years passed before I thought about it seriously.

In 2017, we exhibited at FLAsia in Singapore, the biggest and most renowned franchising and licensing expo in Asia. We were serious about international expansion and were looking to land at least one deal here. We had a lot of interest from potential partners from multiple countries, but they all pointed to a photo of the A1 reformer machine and asked the same question: "Are they your own machines?" When we told them about how we customize a generic machine on the market, their interest wandered straight away. "Too easy to copy. Everyone will try to copy you in Asia—you need your own machine to make it hard for them. Let me know when you have your own machine, and we can talk again." I realized then that until we created a KX reformer machine, we could kiss the idea of successful international expansion goodbye.

Our training method was different, our brand was different, our fitness experience and culture were different, but our machines were generic. They didn't fit. Having our own machines would also fix copycat studios opening around the corner from any of our locations. Well, they could open near us, but they wouldn't be able to follow us into the niche we'd create for ourselves.

At the time, BB was not interested in working with us. They were in the business of generic reformers for the global and, more specifically, traditional Pilates market. So, we began the hunt for manufacturers. First, we tried a local Australian manufacturer that could not adapt to our needs. Then we looked at another US manufacturer, but they were too busy pumping out generic machines—similar to BB—for the vast American Pilates market. They could not give us a prototype fast enough. Then, a Chinese manufacturer who specialized in reformer customizations contacted me out of the blue. He had a proven track record working with an established company in the US with fifty studios and more than 500 hybrid machines.

Creating a machine specifically for the KX workout would be a game changer.

This conversation developed, and the first KX custom reformer, later renamed the "KXformer" project began. Eighteen months later, with more than 300 emails, 1,000 WhatsApp messages, and over $150,000 invested, Andi and I took a week out to visit the factory in Guangzhou, China. We reviewed three prototypes: the KXformer Version 1 (V1), V2, and V3.

The V1

The first prototype was too long, too bulky, and not very nice to look at. It was still a great machine but not for KX, so I gifted it to my dad, who then gifted it to my sister, so let's say it's still in the family!

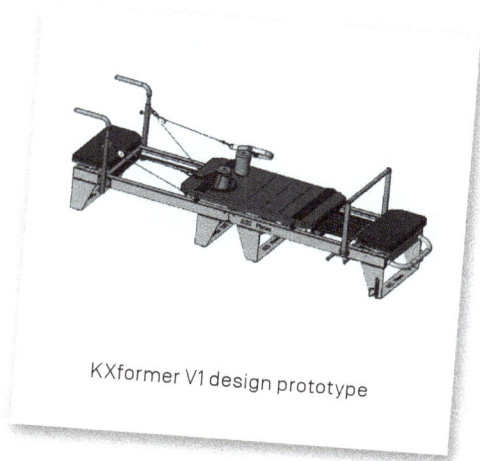

KXformer V1 design prototype

The V2

The second prototype was hot off the manufacturing line when Andi and I landed in China. When we arrived at the factory, we were first taken on a tour that finished in their showroom where the V2 sat under a red cloth. Once it was revealed, the design and manufacturing team were ready with pens and paper so we could provide feedback on what we did and didn't like.

Feeling quite uncomfortable, we politely asked them to leave the room. I'm sure they expected us to be there for thirty minutes, but, for the next eight hours, Andi and I relentlessly went through the machine from top to bottom. It then took us another three hours via translation to explain everything we wanted to change.

KXformer V2, China, 2019

The V3

Although I was always open to change, I was hopeful that the KXformer V3 would be the final prototype.

We had the V3 shipped just in time to launch at the 2019 KX conference—a surprise reveal that our Franchise Partners never saw coming. My keynote finished with the launch of the new dumbbells and accessories, after which we moved into a second room for drinks where the accessories were on show. Then, we unveiled the V3 prototype.

I discussed the design patents that protected our new machine, how we had adapted and changed what we hated about the A1 and A2, and how we had addressed these issues in the new design. I then listed the 20+ new features of the V3 that would specifically enhance the KX workout.

Some Franchise Partners were silent; others shrieked with excitement, and a few cried in fear of more change. All completely acceptable reactions. It's one thing to launch a new product at the core of your business to stave off copycats, but it's also an understandably hard pill to swallow that you'll have to reinvest north of $100,000 back into your business over the next 3–5 years.

We chose to launch the V3 on the first night of our three-day conference. This meant that we could discuss queries and concerns with Franchise Partners over the week.

And man, did we listen.

I believe this moment was a turning point for "fence sitters" who didn't know where their future lay with KX. They would have to decide to either recommit to KX for at least another five years or get out now.

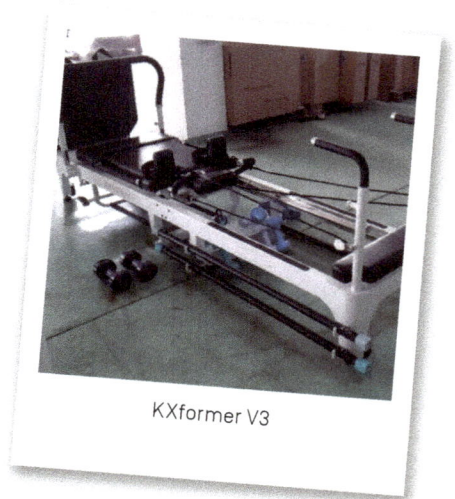

KXformer V3

The V3 was on show throughout the conference and then lived at HQ, where visiting Franchise Partners and Trainers had a chance to play around on it. We collected feedback and then launched the improved V3 for testing in four company studios, so fifty-five machines went into the market.

Although the new machines were a little intimidating, clients loved the look of them and adapted quickly. They hit the mark in bringing KX's updated brand and studio look and feel to life. It was amazing to show our clients that we were putting time and money into improving their workouts and giving them more. It showed that we were innovating and changing for the better. It also showed the Pilates industry and our competitors that we were ahead of the curve and took our workout to the next level.

With the KXformer V3s now in play, clients could no longer go to a KX copycat studio with an ex-KX trainer and get the same workout on the same machine.

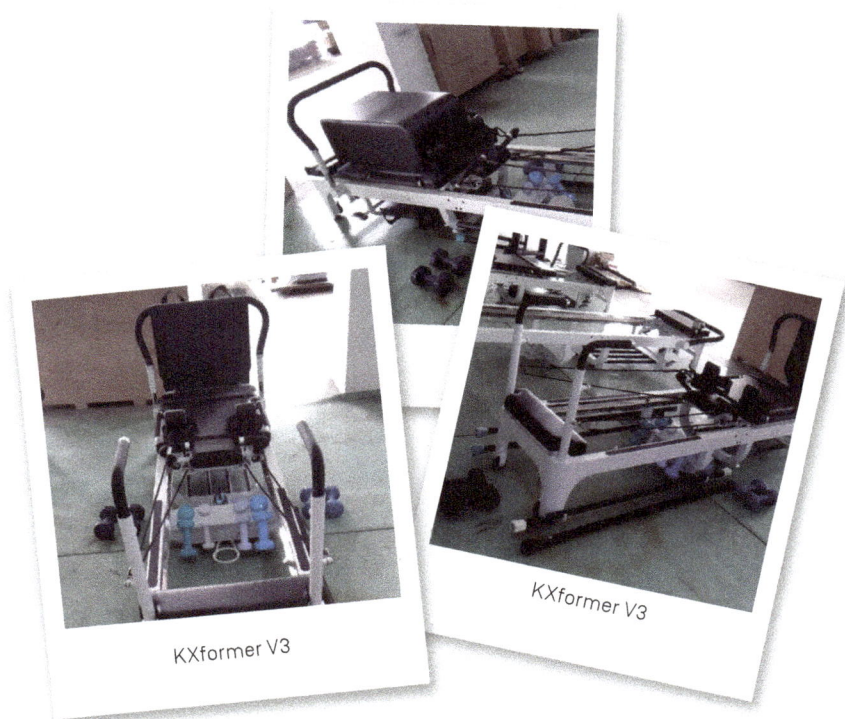

KXformer V3

KXformer V3

BUT...AND THERE IS ALWAYS A BUT

I learned from firsthand experience that when trying to innovate, there are even more "buts" than you'd expect!

Although the new accessories were a breath of fresh air, they came with their own set of issues.

Before we collaborated with Balanced Body on our Pilates rings, we had an initial batch manufactured from China that went into all studios in mid-2019. In the first four weeks of release, we had about seven of them break. I had never heard of a Pilates ring breaking before. Thankfully, no one was hurt! Even though 7 in 1,000 (0.7%) is still a very low number, we could not risk the safety of our clients. So, we recalled them all. A $40,000 lesson right there, as most studios had thrown out or given away their old generic BB rings. We had to purchase generic rings from Balanced Body Australia to allow studios to continue business as usual.

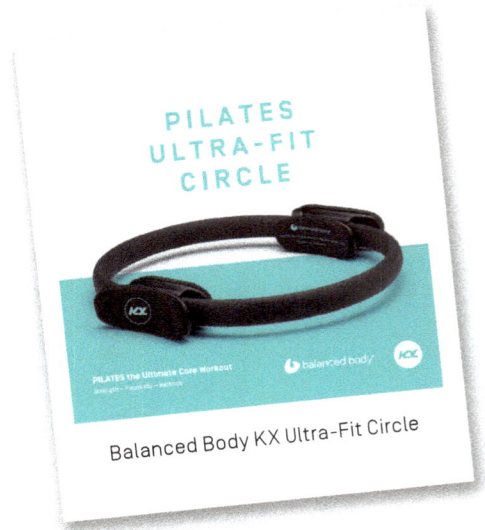

Balanced Body KX Ultra-Fit Circle

Twelve months later, after the collaboration with Balanced Body was complete, we launched the new BB-KX Ultra-Fit Circle.

Pole Faults

Next on the fault list were the plastic caps on our weighted poles. Due to the manufacturing adhesive used and the excessive heat that comes with shipping through hot climates, when the poles started being used in the studios, the rubber KX logos on the end caps came off. Although a minor issue to solve, it looked unprofessional and eventually cost an enormous amount to send technicians out to each studio to adhere every one of them back on correctly. We ultimately changed the entire design on the end caps and produced one mold, so it would never happen again.

Bad Balls

Then there were the toning balls that came too inflated with the wrong valve fitted, so it was challenging to deflate them to the desired squishiness. And last but not least, our new custom-colored 1 kg and 2 kg dumbbells were too light in the chosen KX color, so, after a while, the client's natural body oils ended up staining the handgrips. All were minor, annoying issues that would be eradicated with new and improved versions and colors. But the amount of time, energy, and money wasted was excruciating, not to mention high stress levels, sleepless nights, constant disappointment, and embarrassment.

> *"There is no such thing as failure; you either succeed or you learn."*
> —Kevin Kruse

So let's just say 2019 was a massive year of learning!

REFORMER REVOLUTION

I wish I could keep talking about how magnificent the KXformer V3 trial and testing went. Still, it wasn't long until we realized that the manufacturing quality was not up to our demanded standard.

The design was great, but the quality of raw materials used was flawed, and time and time again, minor niggly issues would come up. From the hardness of the padding to the smoothness of the carriage rollers—there was always an issue that we seemed to be fixing. We had never come across problems with Balanced Body, which meant we had to spend a lot of time and money getting the machines in the market up to scratch. But they were never going to be up to scratch to launch Australia-wide, let alone internationally. Thankfully, we only tried them in company studios. This helped manage expectations, address the client feedback loop quickly, and fix the issues as soon as possible. Using a car analogy, I always said that if we were previously driving a Holden, the V3 looked like a Porsche but, sadly, was built like a Hyundai.

I was extremely disappointed and so devastated. We had taken the quality of the Allegro A1 for granted, and, although the look of them was a bit outdated, for ten years, they had been a fantastic apparatus to our workout. We had come close, just not close enough. But I was not going to be beaten!

Once again, in life, timing is everything.

While communication had started with a new major Pilates manufacturer in China—who had much more of a proven track record in the generic Pilates market— discussions kicked back in with Balanced Body.

Originally, in 2017, the KX business—at just thirty-five studios— was not substantial enough to change their generic manufacturing line to incorporate a customized machine. However, in late 2019, things were different. We were now at seventy studios, doubling the Australian business in three years, with more growth to achieve. We were making enough noise in the Pilates space for them to realize that a project like this would be worth their while. Not to mention the potential loss of losing their number one Australian Pilates Reformer customer.

We had three options:

1. Create a hybrid machine from the current A1 model we had been using.

2. Create a hybrid machine from the new A2 model in the market.

3. Create a brand-new machine from scratch.

Although the idea of making a brand-new machine from scratch was appealing, the thought of going back to the drawing board was not. It would cost a ton of money and likely take 2–3 years to test, manufacture, and trial until we got it right. And even then, we wouldn't know if we were on the right track.

We ruled out option three as time and money were luxuries we no longer had. The track record of the A1 and A2 in the market ticked the box for quality and aesthetics. So, we had made a prototype created for both the A1 and A2.

One big learning from creating the China KXF-V1/V2/V3 was that I overcomplicated the process by wanting too much.

If you add a new feature, something else on the machine needs to adjust to accommodate it. Newton's third law, "For every action, there is an equal and opposite reaction," proved very true here! So, we simplified what we loved on the KXF-V3, took the best parts, and left behind the "niceties that weren't necessities," such as dumbbells and weighted pole racks.

We made both prototypes early in 2020. When I saw them, I knew that we were onto something incredible. The A2 prototype was nicer to look at and had stronger and longer patent protection. We agreed that it was the right one for KX. Twelve months later, we launched the new **"Balanced Body KXformer! (BB-KXF)."**

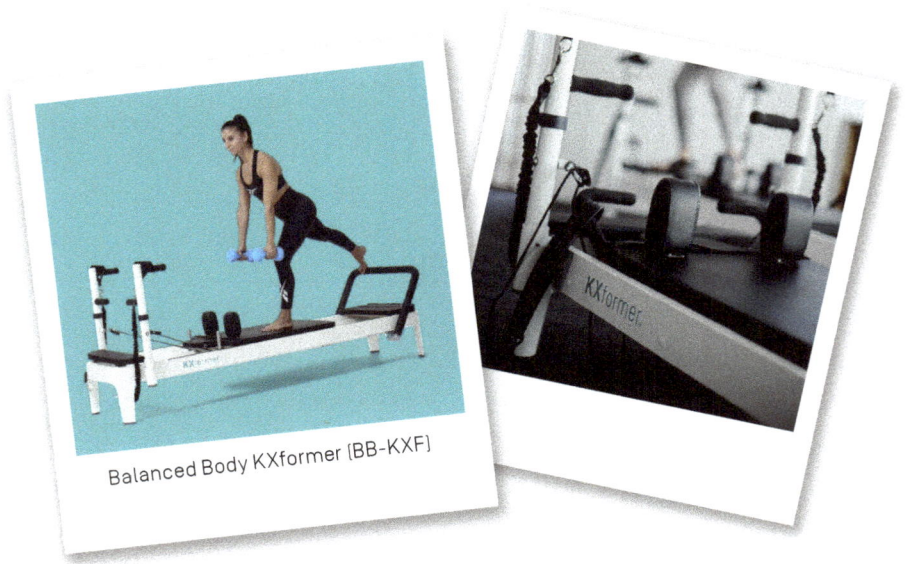

Balanced Body KXformer [BB-KXF]

Why is the Balanced Body KXformer so Different?

For the new KXformer, we added rotatable planking handles and a small platform to the top end of the machine, additional resistance straps, and a new lighter orange spring into the resistance mix. These four features alone add more than twenty exercises to the KX repertoire.

The extended platform on the bottom end makes this machine safer, and custom carbon fiber fabric and the KXformer logo on the side make the machine look incredible and stand out from the rest.

After investing so much into our machine, we had to make sure it was protected and couldn't be copied. Balanced Body was incredibly passionate about protecting their equipment too and had patents out on almost everything they had ever created. Anyone who had tried to copy their equipment was swiftly dealt with.

I had already protected the China KXF-V3 design with patents and trademarked the name KXformer. Since the inception of Balanced Body in 1976, their Founder and CEO, Ken Endelman, had never signed an exclusive agreement. After a lot of convincing, five months of negotiations, and hefty legal bills, we finally came to an exclusive agreement for the BB-KXF. Yeeewwwww!

Developing the KXformer was incredible, frustrating, challenging, embarrassing (at times), and, ultimately, the most rewarding thing I have worked on since starting KX. Was it worth it? Absolutely.

GOING GLOBAL—A WORK IN PROGRESS

The whole intention of KX Pilates' growth plan was to cultivate our kaizen philosophy: small and ongoing improvement.

We've been careful not to completely saturate the market to maintain the brand's exclusive feel and keep the quality experience consistent.

In 2017, we started to put a long-term plan in place. Our mapping and demographic tools put KX Pilates in up to 150+ locations around Australia. In 2023, the network reached one hundred studios and continues to grow at approximately fifteen studios per year. That means we're likely to reach our current Australian expansion goals by 2027. Although, it's hard to predict exactly where the industry will be in the future.

We Began Planning our International Expansion

However, we didn't just want to put "KX dots on the map." It's easy to have one studio in one country and another studio in another so you can say your business is international. Our strategy was to enter an international market and open multiple studios (minimum fifteen) via a Master/ Regional Franchise model. This meant finding a business partner(s) who didn't just want to open one studio, but many, either by themselves as company-owned studios or as a sub-franchisor in that country or region.

Because of its proximity, Asia was number one on our radar.

Although lagging behind the fitness trends of Australia, the UK, and the USA, it was an attractive region. We needed to find a partner on the ground that understood KX while navigating the different cultural, socio-economic, and country laws. An expert in that country was vital.

In 2017, around the time we exhibited at the Singapore FLAsia expo, we met Regita "Tata" Cahyani from Indonesia. Tata is an incredible woman and also strongly in love with our brand. Loving fitness and Pilates, she was born and raised in Jakarta, had lived in Melbourne for six years, and had key political and social connections in her country. We secured our very first international regional franchise deal, and our first international studio opened in Jakarta in August 2018, with a growth plan of many more to come.

Next was China

In 2019, we were headhunted by a Chinese fitness entrepreneur named Tony Xu, based out of Shanghai. He had contacts on the ground in Australia who had done their research into all the boutique fitness companies and was interested in KX, believing it to be the best fit for mass growth in the Greater China region.

However, instead of a master/regional franchise deal, we agreed on a joint venture (JV) deal—more upside for us but a lot more work. With 1.4 billion people in China, the discussions quickly went beyond one hundred studios. The scale Tony talked about always blew our minds. A much more mature market, China already had a huge following in the big box gym space as well as boutique fitness studios for yoga and personal training, but reformer Pilates was yet to take off. The local entrepreneur saw this gap in the Chinese market and was impressed with KX's journey—one they intend to continue. Our first China studio opened in Shanghai in late 2020, with the plan for many more to come.

It wasn't long after our China deal that our JV partner, Tony, got to work, not only to grow KX in China but also to take control of the Greater China region. Under our JV, additional master franchise deals were soon struck for Hong Kong (China), Macau (China), and Taiwan (China), with flagship studios opening in Taiwan (China) in late 2022, Hong Kong (China) in early 2023 and Macau (China) in the works. The future is incredibly bright when it comes to KX in Greater China!

Next—New Zealand!

The KX New Zealand expansion was just perfect timing with the perfect partners. One of the few things we can thank COVID for! Let me explain.

Pre-COVID, Kara Spice was a Trainer at KX Melbourne CBD. A dancer by trade, she was in between contracts at Disneyland Paris, so she was working her way up the Trainer ranks at KX. Being a Kiwi herself, when COVID hit and her specific work visa meant no Australian government support, she was forced to return home to her mother country of NZ. The time spent back home was a blessing in disguise. She connected with family and friends and fell in love with not just her country once again, but her partner, Josh, too. It was as if it was all meant to be.

The only thing missing for her was her affection for KX—and KX studios to match. She always wanted a studio of her own, and it wasn't long until conversations were struck with both her father, Allan, and partner, Josh, about obtaining the master franchise rights for NZ. Kara's love of Pilates and KX, Allan's years of business, financial, and prior franchise experience, and Josh's background in health and fitness education seemed like the perfect partnership. The first NZ studio opened in late 2022, and we can't wait for KX to thrive in our sister country of New Zealand.

Our main focus remains within Australia, growing our national network; however, international inquiry is at an all-time high. It's not the inquiry that excites us, but the quality of leads that are wanting to grow

KX in their cities and countries: Japan, Singapore, and Canada, just to name a few. Our business landscape is now so diverse, navigating cultural boundaries, language barriers, and international law, which may prove challenging but at the same time, so rewarding. KX Pilates does not discriminate. It can be there to assist anybody, in any country, in any language. It's about building a brand that people love no matter what country they are from. It's about personal connection, providing an incredible fitness experience, and changing lives for the better. Our methods are timeless, and our teachings are endless. It's only a matter of time before we see KX Pilates going global, helping as many people as we can.

Signing KX China JV, June 2019

KX New Zealand Master Franchisors
Kara Spice and Josh Gascoigne,
November 2020

KX Pilates Taichung Sanmin,
Taiwan (China), 2022

Jeffrey Shih, Taiwan (China)
Master Franchise Partner, 2022

Regita 'Tata' Cahyani, Indonesian
Master Franchise Partner, August 2018

LESSONS LEARNED

1. Excitement and motivation come and go. Neither is enough to attract continuous success. You need passion, courage, and relentless discipline to succeed, no matter what the cost.

2. Innovate within your brand, not outside of it. This was a huge learning curve for me. The focus of KX's innovations department is, "How can we grow and get better within the current scope of our business?"

3. To innovate effectively, you need to accept that the outcome may not always be a success, and you need to be okay with that outcome.

———

PART THREE

AND THEN THERE WAS COVID

"When everything is uncertain, everything that is important becomes clear."

—Unknown

Chapter 9

WE NEVER PLANNED FOR A PANDEMIC...

2020 started as the best year of my life. I'm not saying it to boast—I promise. I say it as a reminder of where the unprecedented year of 2020 began.

In January, I was on a plane to Vail, Colorado, USA, for a six-week luxury snow adventure, where I'd be surrounded by family and friends.

Returning to Vail was a significant event. It was a reminder of who I was when I started: a ski bum without a clue. I always said that I would return to the slopes, whether KX was a success or failure, and this trip was a hard-earned reward for ten years of KX.

Life in Vail was picturesque. We rented a chalet big enough for the four of us and visiting friends and family to pass through. Every day was a beautiful, snowy adventure. My son Archer, who had only just turned four, fell in love with skiing on this trip. After six weeks on the slopes, he was nailing the blue runs. Ava, who was just two and a half, was old enough to figure out she preferred snowboarding and stuck to the bunny hill.

At the same time, KX was smashing it. We had twelve new studios to open, and year-on-year growth was tracking at ten percent. Selina was finding her groove as the CEO, and I was stepping further away from the day-to-day operations. We'd completed the setup and held the first meetings with the KX external advisory board, made up of franchise founders and seasoned business leaders. Their advice helped us make big decisions, including adding four studios to our company portfolio, bringing it from seven to eleven.

It was February when the news of COVID was spreading—fast.

We were lucky to travel when we did. We left on February 8, and all the American ski resorts closed just four weeks later.

TEN YEARS OF KX

February 2020 was a big one for KX: ten years in business.

We returned from Colorado and rushed to Sydney to attend the annual KX Conference. We had an exceptional lineup of motivational speakers—the room was packed—and it was by far the best KX Conference we'd ever had. It was a proud moment to be part of KX.

KX 10 year anniversary super yacht celebrations with our best friends

The venue, funnily enough, was Sydney's Quarantine Station in Manly. We were overlooking Sydney Harbour with forty Franchise Partners, our key suppliers, and loyal HQ team, inspiration oozing and positive energy flowing.

Sydney's weather turned it on for us—such a treat from Melbourne! We celebrated our momentous ten-year milestone with a boat party on a one-hundred-passenger super yacht for the entire KX team, friends, and family.

What a feeling that was, cruising around Sydney Harbour on a super yacht. Then came the crush of COVID.

COVID SHOCK

On Sunday March 22, 2020, at 8 pm, KX Pilates studios were among the first group of recreation centers and gyms to be told to close their doors. At noon the next day, under stage three ruling by the Australian Federal Government, all sixty-seven KX studios were shut.

I remember the sinking feeling in my gut as I stared at the TV, watching the press conference unfold. I looked over at Andi in total shock and disbelief. I couldn't grasp the fact that every one of our KX studios would have to close. And we had no idea for how long. I was completely devastated.

Would this closure mean that the last ten years of tireless days and nights, hours upon hours of dedication, sweat, time, and energy would be for nothing?

For the first time in my life, I felt like someone—or something—was controlling me. I felt helpless. Being somewhat of a control freak, my anxiety soared.

My parents called me straight after the news announcement to provide their unwavering support. There were few words to describe what was happening. I asked, "In forty-five years of being in business, Dad, how many days did you close?"

His reply? "Just one, son, for a renovation." Wow. Neither recent history nor almost fifty years of business experience could help.

Since KX's inception in 2010, we had only ever shut a KX Pilates studio door for half a day for a studio refurb. Unlike other fitness companies who would close one day a week or on public or religious holidays, I had an unspoken promise from the very beginning that we would be there for our clients every day, 24/7, 365 days a year.

This was not in the plan. How could we help people define themselves if we couldn't have people in the studio? I still remember the crisis conference call later that night with Selina and Andi, and I (regretfully) said, "Oh well, if we have to close, we have to close—and there is not much more we can do."

I woke up the next day in a different world. We all did. And I realized what a ridiculous statement I had made. There was just so much we could do and needed to do—now. We quickly shifted into "getting shit done" mode, something Andi and I had become accustomed to over the years. If there was one thing I could bring to this situation, it was resilience and a positive mindset.

The next day, the entire HQ team went into BEAST mode. The marketing team ramped up content and communications to our network and clients. Our systems and training team worked to create an online KX workout experience through the KX App. Our finance team tightened spending, cutting every expense they could, pushing out creditors, and quickly forward planning cash flow scenarios. Simultaneously, the company studio team started exploring how to lease our reformer machines to clients in their homes.

Our strategy to the Executive Team was clear:

STAY AFLOAT.

STAY RELEVANT.

STAY CONNECTED.

AND HUSTLE LIKE WE HAVE NEVER HUSTLED BEFORE!

KX's revenue took an immediate ninety-eight percent hit, so "stay afloat" was the priority. We also knew that we had to find a way to stay connected to our clients. They had to know we were there and, importantly, that we were all—our clients, Trainers, Franchise Partners, and the HQ team—in this together.

LOCKDOWN 1.0

Lockdown 1.0 went for ten or eleven weeks for most states.

Victoria—home to over thirty KX studios, accounting for more than fifty percent of our business—had the longest lockdown in Australia at thirteen weeks. During this time, we banded together. Our Franchise Partners and Trainers utilized a "KX Champions" Facebook group, a place for positive affirmations, banter, fitness challenges, and trainer group workouts. We worked closely with our newly appointed Emotional Fitness Coach, Joe Pane (@joepaneinsights), to work through the individual challenges that COVID presented us and create an open dialogue that it is "OK not to be OK."

It was vital for our clients to continue their fitness journey even if our studios were closed. We launched "KX Life," our KX App, which was our online "KX At Home" workout portal, to suit clients on every budget. "Freemium" provided free, on-demand classes. "Premium" was just $5/

week, which provided new on-demand classes every day. This would eventually become our "anytime library" of 90+ at-home twenty-minute workouts.

We rolled these options out quickly, but they lacked the personalized experience for which KX is famous. That's when we introduced LIVE At Home workouts via Zoom. For forty-five minutes, you could get your butt kicked with the assistance of two instructors on-screen: a demonstrator and the primary trainer, who instructed the class, focused on correcting technique, throwing out banter, and bringing some of the "in-studio" KX experience to clients' homes. These were a massive hit for the majority of our closed studios.

To say that this "pivot"—I hate that word, but it was a business-saving pivot—was stressful and manic would be an understatement. There were tears, midnight finishes, early starts, a lot of screaming, and that was just my day! We focused on "controlling the controllable" and always referencing that "we are all in this together." I was grateful to be part of a franchise at this point, to feel the solidarity among the network; it was comforting, and most of our Franchise Partners felt the same.

They were later recognized for their sacrifice and hard work, but they didn't know that would be the case at the time.

We asked a lot of the HQ team during this time. When we closed all our studios, the team dropped back to two days a week, but their full-time workload continued. The team soldiered on, supporting the studios and getting on with it. I was, and continue to be, in awe of every single one of them.

In early June, gyms and fitness centers were given the go-ahead to open again. There was anxious energy about reopening. The world had changed; COVID was still in our community. Would our KXers be keen to get back or cautious about returning?

The response to opening was overwhelming, helped by our "Reignite Your Routine" campaign. Clients, new and old, rushed into the studios.

People were still working from home, so our daytime classes filled up. The lines had blurred to the previous "before and after work" peak class times. We added more classes, so capacity increased, which saw a boost of 20–55 percent in sales from the previous year. By the end of June, KX studios all over the country were buzzing.

Three weeks later, our freedom in Melbourne was ripped out from under us—again.

LOCKDOWN 2.0

On July 8, 2020, a hotel quarantine bungle saw Melbourne and the Mitchell Shire (a large section of regional Melbourne) back into lockdown. Stage four restrictions were severe:

- Face masks mandatory outside of the home
- No visitors—at all
- 8 pm–5 am curfew
- Only leave home for four reasons: one hour per day exercise; essential work (approved workers only); essential shopping; caregiving, medical and compassionate grounds
- Must stay within a 5 km radius of your home
- And the worst of all—ALL PLAYGROUNDS CLOSED!

This lockdown was later acknowledged as one of the longest and harshest in the world, lasting a total of 112 days.

As a business born in Melbourne, there were thirty-five KX studios in the state—more than half of our entire network. It sucked that so many had to close again, but at the same time, we were grateful that the other half were able to stay open and continued to be busy.

It wasn't just our Melbourne Franchise Partners who were doing it tough; our entire HQ Team went through the wringer. Every time a state changed the rules or experienced another "COVID outbreak scare," the HQ team responded with its crisis and communications plan. I can't tell you how many times we shut doors in one state while reopening them in another.

The pressure on our HQ team in Melbourne was relentless. Every time a state or local area went into lockdown, the KX HQ team went into BEAST mode to action the huge number of tasks to support our Franchise Partners.

At the time of writing, Victoria just entered a sixth lockdown, and Australia has been in and out of lockdowns for over eighteen months. It was and still is relentless, and our Franchise Partners' needs were always high, placing huge demand on our already stretched and stressed team.

Within any franchise, there are always high expectations placed on senior leaders and the HQ team. We rely on their expertise and experience to do the job well. But add the stress of a "once in one hundred years pandemic" to the mix, an overnight change to our business model—from in-person to online—and we felt the pain.

We were never going to get it one hundred percent right. But the team did an incredible job, and I saw first-hand the dedication, discipline, and incredible work that went into keeping the company afloat. It was touch and go for a while. We had to dip into our overdraft just to stay afloat, but we continued to get through it.

To this day, I'm not sure that our network will truly understand the lengths the team went to. Could it have been done better? Of course. But the team did the best they could with their skillset and the limited resources they had, and they did it while continuing to support the studios that could open and juggling the stress of their personal lives while in lockdown. It was so tough for everyone.

Burnout and screen fatigue were genuine, and, for a lot of understand-able reasons, we said goodbye to many HQ members at the end of 2020. I will forever be grateful to our COVID HQ Team. Without them, we would not have survived the year of 2020. So, if any of them are reading this, I'll repeat it. THANK YOU.

LOVE IN LOCKDOWN

There is one absolute certainty of living through a global pandemic—nothing is certain! I certainly didn't predict that I would fall in love with my wife all over again.

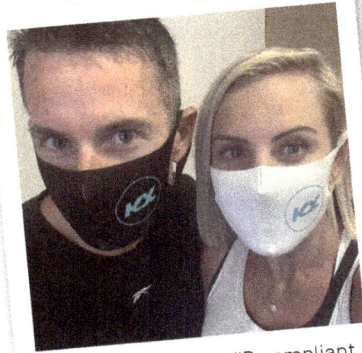

Andi and I being COVID compliant

Let me tell you about my wife, Andi. She is the person who sees the solution to a problem before you've even finished the conversation. It can be annoying, sometimes (sorry, lover, but it's true). She's also the person who always helps others and never asks for any praise or thanks in return. When there's an extreme deadline to meet or a crisis of global proportions, Andi operates at her peak. It's like the energy propels her forward, and she gains extreme clarity and precision in making decisions. I've never appreciated her more than I did in 2020.

I just knew that by having Andi by my side, things would be OK, no matter what happened. There was nothing she wouldn't do to make sure that KX survived, and her love for what we had built together was unstoppable. So, at the beginning of 2020, while we were still gathering our thoughts and shouting profanity, Andi discussed adapting the KX workout online and talking to our tech partner, Hapana, about how to make it happen—fast. Andi was the one who made sure we could do it and knew that we needed to deliver and communicate with our network. She rallied the troops at HQ to make it happen.

At the time, Andi was KX's Head of Systems, but, in truth, no one knew the ins and outs of **KX** better than she. A colleague once described Andi as the **KX** Oracle (Andi hated that), but there was no denying her ability to get shit done. Over the years, Andi stepped into the roles the business needed at the time: reception, marketing, operations, data analytics…you name it; Andi did it. The annoying thing is that she did it all well. When the pandemic changed everything, we soon learned that, again, Andi would do whatever was needed.

So, when stage four restrictions came into effect for a second lockdown, we decided that I would stay home with our two kids, and Andi would focus her energy on **KX**.

KIDS AND LOCKDOWN

I'll be honest; staying at home full-time with the kids was daunting. I've always been a hands-on dad, and I grew up in a big family, but this was different. Kindergarten and childcare were closed. We couldn't visit anyone. How would I keep my very energetic

The Burnley (VIC) Train Bridge was a popular COVID hangout with Archer and Ava

three- and four-year-old kids entertained when I could only go outside for a single hour each day?

We maximized our outdoor time and got both kids learning to ride their bikes without training wheels. Ava was just three years old when she decided she was going to ride a two-wheeler. In three minutes, she was off and never looked back. Her mother's stubbornness and competitiveness drive her. Ahem.

Archer had learned to ride a bike in the first lockdown, so now family bike rides were a daily focus.

One hour goes by very quickly with two small kids on bikes. I cannot confirm nor deny that we stuck to just an hour—but let's just say that indoor arts and crafts is not my forte.

Over the 112 days, the kids and I would go on a different adventure every day. We'd explore parks, nature reserves, and local abandoned warehouses; we'd climb underneath bridges, search for "friendly bears" along the Yarra River, and make tree and cubby houses out of sticks and branches in the local bushland of urban reserves. We also found the Melbourne University Horticultural Campus, which was quickly renamed the "Enchanted Forest," with its winding paths, plants, trees, streams, and waterfalls that we lost ourselves in daily. We would hunt for and find amazing trees to climb, build amateur bike paths and jumps, and head to the post office frequently to send chocolates, paintings, and drawings to friends and family.

Unlike the previous year, the Melbourne Winter of 2020 was kind and not that wet, so we really did get outside every day. Neither of the kids were at school yet, so, unlike many of our friends, we didn't have to battle homeschooling.

THE ISO-BEARD COMPETITION

It's funny the things you come up with in the middle of a pandemic. After a brief discussion with four of my best mates, the "iso-beard" competition began in June 2020. A substantial financial punishment would occur for anyone who ever trimmed his beard!

Apart from showing my gray/white hair and looking a lot older, the beard itch was real. There

Iso-Beard Challenge (I lost!)

was not a day that went past where I didn't want to shave. I lasted five months and used the end of lockdown to "come clean," so to speak. So, unfortunately, "Santa," as I was aptly named, did not make it to Xmas!

ISO-FIT, ISO-QUIT

When going into a second lockdown after only just coming out of one three weeks earlier, I looked at what I wanted to do differently.

Growing a beard, quitting drinking, and prioritizing fitness were all top of the list. I didn't touch a drop of alcohol in lockdown 2.0, and I trained six days a week and was extremely strict with my diet. My body had never felt better, and I was probably the fittest and healthiest I had been in a decade.

My role at home helped my relationship, too. Our marriage had never been better. Because our roles were clear, we both supported each other one hundred percent—we just focused on getting through together. Things were going so well that the discussion got to "let's have another baby!" So, I canceled my planned vasectomy—too much information, I know—and before the end of the second lockdown, we were pregnant with our third child, Amelia Willow Smith, affectionately known as "Millie."

INNOVATION IN COVID TIMES

Even though the KX studios were closed, there was still a lot of momentum for international growth.

We signed a joint venture agreement in China with a leading fitness and business personality that would see a plan to open several studios before the end of 2020. With our focus on keeping KX studios in Australia afloat, we decided to give our JV partner, Tony, and his team the freedom to "just do it." From the beginning, Tony made it known that while KX had cult-like status in Australia, making KX a success in China would require a different approach. We'd need to explore "other opportunities" for KX in China outside of the stand-alone studio model that had worked so well for us in Australia. His approach was more "shoot first, ask questions later." This made me understandably nervous, especially when I was all about "crossing our T's and dotting our I's" before any new studio opening.

Regulations, while essential, can be a roadblock to entrepreneurship.

For KX China to succeed, we looked at many complementary business options. Education, postnatal and rehabilitation Pilates, and licensing models to personal training and "big box" gyms were considered. At the time of writing, all these options are being considered, trialed, and tested.

The IP and brand of KX Pilates were protected and gave me the comfort to allow Tony to explore these options. This wouldn't have been possible without a trusting relationship. We had built this in 2018 and 2019 when we could travel, and we visited China to spend time with Tony and his team.

2020 was also when we finalized the new Balanced Body KXformer machine, the "BB-KXF." On the project, I had now spent four years and over $250,000 in research and development of prototypes, testing, time, and energy. It was such a great feeling to see the crisp, white, sexy machines placed into four of our studios in December 2020. The national rollout will be ongoing.

We also managed to open five new studios during 2020, which, in hindsight, is insane but shows that the passion for KX Pilates is strong.

COVID CULTURE

There's no doubt that 2020 was a dog of a year for our Franchise Partners, for everyone.

Although we did our best to maintain a positive outlook during 2020, an ugly feeling erupted from within the network, especially in Victoria, where the lockdown was the longest. In the absence of a structured workday, the gossip mill within the network was rife, and the entire feeling and culture within KX were affected—dramatically.

For the majority of our network, studios were shut with little or no income. When you throw fear and uncertainty and COVID into that mix, shit gets hard, quickly. Connection within the KX network was at an all-time low.

I heard rumors that I had abandoned our KXers and the people that love KX as much as I did because I wasn't the CEO anymore, and I was just waiting for the chance to sell the business. Talk about a slap in the face with a cold fish! The worst thing was that it couldn't have been further from the truth.

The people and the business that I adored were struggling—what could I do to change it?

I started asking questions and with the help of my good friend, Hinda, who was our Head of Marketing during COVID, we realized that our internal communication sucked. This wasn't on purpose or anyone's fault; we thought we were doing "the standard thing." We were focused on running a business, but when the business stopped, it was apparent that our internal communications were nonexistent.

#BELONGTOSOMETHINGBETTER

You might have guessed that I am not the kind of person who sits back and does nothing.

I wanted to call out the negativity, the toxicity, and the rumors. I wanted to address that we've had an internal communications problem since the inception of KX.

So, late in 2020, when studios could reopen, I made a video to address these issues with our network. Together with the HQ team, I owned our mistakes, our flaws, and talked about the positives we had achieved and what was to come. Large, in-person meetings weren't allowed, but we held Zoom calls to talk about the challenges, what was needed, and collaborate.

That's about the time I took responsibility for being the Chief Cultural Officer, kicked off another video to share this vision, and started the internal movement: #belongtosomethingbetter.

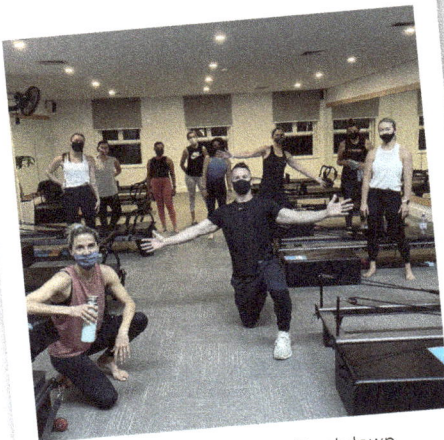

Midnight class out of lockdown

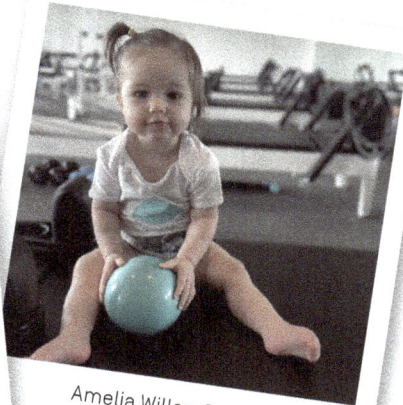

Amelia Willow Smith, AKA Millie

The movement was about improving our internal comms and sharing transparently, but it was important to give people a choice. The next chapter of KX is about to begin. Let's continue this journey together. KX had just turned ten! We had our fair share of mistakes to own, but our focus was to grow the business. The next ten-year focus is to grow our people.

I threw myself at my new role with everything I had. I wanted to help our Franchise Partners and unite the team again. We started working closely with Greg Nathan and the Franchise Relationship Institute to find out what we were doing well, what we were not doing well, and to assist us. Whether you were from HQ or were a single- or multi-site Franchise Partner, we would grow and develop as people together.

To bring back the buzz, we decided to organize studio visits and "Classes with the Founder." We would also write internal articles on culture and how we could all improve, and we would interview our Franchise Partners and external experts who we felt could add value to our network.

Maintaining and uplifting culture in KX will always be a focus point moving forward. It is and still will be a work in progress. But I'm feeling confident and more passionate about our people than ever, and I want them to achieve their goals and reach their full potential.

LESSONS LEARNED

1. It was difficult not knowing when any of it was going to end. I learned to **take one day at a time**.

2. **Certainty is an illusion.** Some people need it to feel secure, but the more you get used to the fact that nothing in life is certain, the more resilient and prepared you will be.

3. You can never prepare for the worst, but you can *mentally* **prepare for the worst**! Business has shown me some of life's highest highs and lowest lows. The more you understand that it's not a matter of how, but when things will go belly up, the quicker you will get your headspace in the position it needs to be to overcome it.

4. **It's OK to get angry**, scream F*CK YOU to the world, be scared, and freak out. But do it quickly, get back up on your feet, and keep moving.

5. **Don't put all your eggs in one basket.** We were grateful that we had studios all around the country and that we had diversified our offer.

6. **Know what is important and what is just noise.** If COVID taught me anything, it was how incredibly important and precious my family and friends are to me. Sure, business, KX, and making money are good, but they mean nothing compared to those closest to you. I treasure them more, and although I am very proud of what we have achieved with KX, I am prouder of what Andi and I have achieved together as a partnership, and the family we have created.

PART FOUR

THE LONG AND WINDY FRANCHISE JOURNEY

"Franchising is a powerful tool to help people gain financial independence, express their drive to achieve in creative ways, and put something back into the community."

—Greg Nathan

Chapter 10

THE KX FRANCHISE JOURNEY

FRANCHISING IN AUSTRALIA

Did you know, per capita, Australia is the most franchised country in the world? Bakers Delight, Endota, F45, Boost Juice, Clark Rubber—there are too many to name.

Franchising is when a network of owners opens identical stores, studios, or clinics that follow the same rules and guidelines under the same brand. In return, they pay a royalty fee to the franchise holder. Sounds simple, right? Ha! Growing a successful franchise is not easy.

WHY FRANCHISE?

There are so many ways to franchise your business, and there isn't really a universally agreed "right" way. The key to starting a successful franchise is to choose what is best for you and your business and adapt with your network, business, and community. Did I mention the importance of being adaptive?

If you are a business owner looking to expand your empire through franchising, ask yourself, "Why?"

Franchising is not a way to get rich quickly. Quite the opposite, in fact: slow and steady is key to building a successful franchise. However, the return you will see should outweigh the time it has taken you to get there.

For me, franchising was and still is a way to share the KX experience.

If I had not franchised KX, I might have stopped when I had opened ten studios. Financially, it would've been a quicker way to make money. But I wanted to bring the KX experience to as many people as possible. And, later, it was to help people achieve their financial dreams of owning their own business. So, franchising was the right choice for me.

Franchising works well for KX because a lot of our Franchise Partners were originally Trainers or clients. Their love of KX expands to wanting to own a studio of their own. It made sense to help people join our brand

and ultimately get bigger and more successful together instead of pushing them away and eventually turning them into competitors.

WHERE TO START?

If you're in Australia, you should jump on the Franchise Council of Australia (FCA) website and completely engulf yourself in learning everything you can, whether you are a potential franchisor or Franchise Partner. When the time is right, you can become a member. The FCA's entire purpose is to enable you to succeed in the franchise space, so let them.

If you're wanting to start a franchise outside of Australia, you should look up your local equivalent of the FCA for relevant information and assistance.

I attended every single FCA conference or learning event and networked with as many people in the industry as I could. Franchising is a business model, and it doesn't matter what you're selling; you'll experience the same problems, from issues in your network, to marketing, finance, or operational issues. Although your product or service may be different from that of the person sitting next to you, everyone is either experiencing or has experienced what you are or will be going through.

I found that everyone in the Australian franchise industry is so willing to help you succeed, learn, and grow. I learned a lot and appreciated learning from others' mistakes.

In the early days, I was asked to sit on the FCA's Melbourne franchisor board. It was great sitting alongside some of Australia's most well-known and successful franchise networks, which ranged from a start-up of two years, to pioneer businesses that had been around for thirty years or more. I learned so much from CEOs and founders alike.

In 2017, KX Pilates won the FCA's NextGen in Franchising Award and was a finalist for the Emerging Franchisor of the Year, which put KX, and my name, on the map and, in turn, opened doors. People start to recognize you, and they go out of their way to congratulate you and ask how they can assist further, and vice versa. You might even be able to help them. Because of that connection, I've been lucky enough to be asked to judge these awards over the past couple of years. Being an advocate for the franchise industry is hugely beneficial for the long-term success of your business.

At the end of the day, you can, and really should, choose to help the industry progress and move forward. I am now a mentor with an Emerging Franchisors Group, providing advice and support, and assisting up-and-coming franchisors to not make the mistakes I did. I also help in business advisory for some up-and-coming franchisors—which do not compete with KX—in the fitness space.

WHAT KIND OF FRANCHISOR DO YOU WANT TO BE?

From the very beginning, it's essential to decide what type of Franchisor you're going to be. I was very much about being a business partner.

Are You Going to be a Dictator?

A dictator doesn't allow ideas to come through. "You've bought in, now shut up and listen!" In a system like this, you may be able to get things done fast and grow quickly; although, from experience, it's a fast avenue to get Franchise Partners offside.

Are You Going to be a Business Partner?

Is it about the long-term happiness and success of your Franchise Partners? I feel that this is the most successful way to do it, where there's mutual respect and open dialogue so you can advance the brand together.

Our Franchise Partners know they can come and tell me their concerns or how they're feeling, any time, any day, which is a powerful outcome. Most of the time, people just want to be listened to and acknowledged. The best result is when you become ambassadors, not just for the brand but also for each other. I would imagine that if you took a dictator leadership approach, a Franchise Partner would not be an ambassador for you. People don't care how much money they earn if they're not respected. Period.

BE A FRANCHISE AMBASSADOR

Being an ambassador of franchising is important. It shows you care about the industry as a whole and the direction it's going. It will also enable you to connect with great leaders of extensive networks to better your understanding of franchising.

I'm a real advocate for being an ambassador for the franchising industry.

Being an ambassador is being part of the community. Surround yourself with the right people who will help you drive reciprocal benefits. Support the local café, school, or hairdresser that will also support you.

A FRANCHISE TIMELINE: KX PILATES

To give you an idea of the KX franchise journey, the stages of our growth looked something like this:

Years 1–3
Start-up corporate (company studio) stage: three corporate studios open.

- This is where the grind occurred, proving the KX concept, getting the KX brand out there, testing all marketing avenues, learning, and doing every task possible in the business.

- We started with nothing, stayed lean, tested, and measured, then slowly started to see the light at the end of the tunnel and some profit.

Years 3–4
Consolidation: additional three (total six) part-owned corporate studios.

- The initial three studios reached their twenty-four-month business maturity.

- We proved the concept in both one hundred percent company-owned and fifty percent part-owned company models.

- We employed managers and administration staff for support.

- We achieved profit that equaled the return on investment of approximately 3-4 years for future Franchise Partners (but of course there are no guarantees).

Years 4–6

Franchise start-up stage: fifteen franchises sold.

- Initial hiring of franchise staff, including a marketing and business development manager.

- We received good returns here as we ran the franchise on low staff and low expenses, but we still did everything and remained everything to everyone.

- We used the uplift opportunity to move and open **KX** in Sydney, with Andi and I living there for two years.

Years 6–8

Franchise growth stage: additional twenty studios sold (total thirty-five).

- Expenses went through the roof building our head office team: finance, operations, marketing, administration, training, project management, software, rent for a bigger office, etc.

- We went from three full-time staff to twelve and increased the training team from three to ten.

- Good growth, but we went in the negative due to the massive reinvestment into the business to pay for future support to assist with our growth.

- We opened in the Queensland, South Australian, and Western Australian markets.

Years 8–10

Franchise maturation stage: Additional thirty studios sold (total 65+ studios).

- The franchise reaches maturity with consistent growth continuing.

- I stepped down as CEO in November 2018. We had fifty studios, and Selina Bridge was hired.

- We saw profit rise.

- We solidified the head office team and appointed more business performance managers as the network grew.

- We signed our first Regional Development Franchise Agreement and opened our first international franchise studio in Jakarta, Indonesia.

- We opened in Tasmania and the Australian Capital Territory markets, solidifying KX in all states and major cities (except Northern Territory).

Years 10+ Projection

Global expansion: 70–150 studios Australia-wide, 500 studios globally.

- The franchise matures. Royalties are paying for cash flow and expenses without the need for franchise fees coming in. Anything additional should be "blue sky" money.

- We predict an average of approximately fifteen (or more) studios opening up annually in Australia until we reach our estimated cap of 150 over the next five years.

- Cash at the bank is healthy, and money can now be reinvested into innovation and other business units to increase profits for Franchise Partners and the company.

PAUL CICCHETTI—FROM POSTIE TO KX MULTI-STUDIO OWNER @kxpilatesmosman

Paul's Pilates journey started in Perth, Western Australia. He had just finished high school and had not dabbled in many forms of fitness aside from competitive swimming. When he was eighteen years old, his friends were partying hard, but Paul wanted to deviate from that lifestyle and begin building a strong, healthy body. However, the traditional gym environment intimidated him.

Due to his interest in pop culture, he became aware of Pilates through US and UK celebrities. He couldn't believe how amazing some of the older celebs looked. To Paul, Madonna was an idol and an inspiration, and, at fifty years old, she still looked and performed like a thirty-year-old. Growing up gay and closeted in a conservative area, he was searching for a way to build confidence and truly express himself—and he found it.

After looking into Pilates, he saw that he could attend mat group classes in Perth, so he took the leap and booked a session. He recalls how welcoming the environment was, even though he was the only guy there. Surrounded by strong women—both young and mature—he strengthened his core and his mind and began shaping his lanky teenage body into something that looked and felt great. He continued weekly mat sessions for several years while working in different fields, including retail, photography, and hospitality. Over time, he noticed that more and more men, young and old, fit and unfit, novices and athletes, were attending Pilates classes. The gradual shift was fascinating to observe.

In 2014, at age twenty-three, Paul moved to the East Coast of Australia to experience life in the big smoke: the great city of Melbourne. After moving in with friends in Richmond, he discovered KX Pilates. At the time, he was working a couple of jobs: one in his aunt's restaurant and another as a postie. On his postal route, he chose to use a push-bike instead of a motorcycle in order to keep fit. He was studying for his Cert IV in Fitness at the time, so he didn't want to spend the entire work week being (relatively) sedentary.

He recalls the first time he walked upstairs to see what KX Pilates was all about. After examining the "weird-looking machines," he thought: "OK, I need to give this a go." Due to his mat pilates experience, he was able to jump right in and pick up the new workouts quickly. From the start, he was addicted. For the next two years—and beyond!—KX kept him fit and strong.

At the time, Eli and I co-owned the Richmond studio, and when Eli found out that Paul had finished his Cert IV in Fitness, she wasted no time offering him a job as a Trainer at Richmond and the new location opening in Brighton. After he completed his KX Academy training, at age twenty-five, Paul began teaching Pilates.

With Eli and her team cheering him on, Paul flourished as a Trainer. He truly felt that he had found his calling. He was in his element and loved teaching the people of Melbourne. In 2016, after two years as a Trainer, Eli offered Paul the chance to become her business partner. He had never owned a business before, and the proposition was nerve-racking. But once he overcame his initial hesitation, the decision to join Eli in partnership wasn't difficult at all. He already felt super supported by the team, and taking the opportunity to further progress his KX journey simply made sense. He loved doing what he did, helping people build the confidence he wished he'd had when he was younger, and he was excited to harness everything he had learned, and develop as a business owner. Besides, the company was really growing. At that point, it was clear that KX wasn't just a fad, but a solid business model that was here to stay.

After working as a Trainer for years, Paul was ready to take the next step, to start something new. He moved to Sydney to open a studio in Mosman, where he worked with an amazing team of superstar Trainers. He was excited to not only be a Franchise Partner but also to direct his energy into mentoring teams across multiple studios. It's one thing to grow from your experiences, but it's another to help others on their journey. Much of his drive comes from wanting to pass on to others the baton of wellness, confidence, and that feeling of "home" that comes with being a part of the KX family. Paul continued to enjoy the KX lifestyle while thriving on the inspiration and challenges that come with owning and running a business.

Over the years, he has discovered that his superpower is the ability to coordinate incredible in-studio experiences. While his clients always have a fantastic experience, he has an amazing time too. His energy is contagious. Combined with pumping music and challenging exercises, he leaves people forgetting about whatever stressful thoughts were on their mind before walking in the door. He believes in always creating that incredible experience, which is why his studios are so successful. Paul loves doing what he does, and his clients and his team feel it.

He aims to continue nurturing KX communities and open a fourth studio. For anyone who is just opening their first KX studio, he has this advice: "Find a way to continue doing what you love. If you enjoy teaching classes, you need to delegate certain tasks to others and still have the time and energy to mentor your team. If your talent and passion lie in behind-the-scenes work, you need to hire people you can rely on to handle other duties."

"Relationships are also important. If you keep an open heart and mind, you can learn a lot from everyone you encounter." For Paul, KX gave him the confidence to connect with people. Even if he makes a mistake, he knows that he will learn from the experience and grow. From postie to multi-studio owner, Paul shows no signs of slowing down, and he never plans to stop doing KX Pilates.

LESSONS LEARNED

1. Franchising is a long but rewarding journey. It takes consistent hard work.

2. Remember that every business is different. As your business grows and succeeds, the perception might be that you are successful and swimming in dollars, but that might not be the case.

3. In 2019, KX hit $25 million in revenue. Sounds great, right? As an owner, I see eight percent, or $1.7 million, of that. But that paid for fifteen full-time staff, five part-time staff, head office rent, national travel (flights and accommodation), accounting, legal fees—you get the idea. It all adds up. So just remember that the media love reporting on big numbers, and perception is a beautiful thing!

4. For years, and probably even to this day, many of my multi-site Franchise Partners see more profit than the company, just like a football team may be more profitable than the league itself. You need to be completely okay with this. How amazing is it that they are succeeding from the brand you started? In return, you get a loyal brand advocate who will help to grow your brand. You succeed; they succeed—the beautiful symbiotic franchise relationship.

5. The bigger you get, the more problems you will face. If you surround yourself with the right people who understand you and your vision, you're more likely to reach your goals together.

6. One of my favorite sayings is, "You can't get angry or frustrated at people who are uninformed, don't know the full story, or simply don't understand." So, it's your job to inform them, which again highlights the importance of effective communication.

7. If you want to be a profitable owner-operator franchisor, aim to have thirty or more sites for it to be financially worth your while. If you're going to shift away from being on the frontline and grow a larger franchise like KX, then aim for a minimum of seventy sites. Unless you are hitting those numbers, franchising is painful and unrewarding: a lot of effort for very little return.

8. There are financial experts out there who specialize in franchising, and a good accountant can point you in the right direction. As with any advice, I always assess by specialty. Don't use an accountant who does not specialize in franchise accounting or financial modeling for franchise networks. Your business is no different from your health: when general things come up, go to your GP, but when something specific and more complex comes up, go to a specialist. They cost more money, but it's worth it for the specialist advice.

"Follow your passion,
it will lead to your purpose."

—Oprah

Chapter 11

PASSION AND BUSINESS

I get asked a lot of questions about how I started out and the world of franchising in Australia. So, I thought I'd share my "warts and all" thoughts on the topic.

But here is my disclaimer: I have never been a Franchise Partner, nor do I intend to be in the future. This is just my raw, honest opinion that might prompt you to think differently.

My best advice? If you are truly considering the world of franchising, talk to Franchise Partners to find out what it's *really* like to take ownership in that specific brand.

FIRST, WHAT'S YOUR PASSION?

Do you want to be an owner/operator? Do you see yourself in the business full time, 40+ hours a week? Is it something you want to do part-time? Or are you considering a franchise purely from an investor point of view? Consider your involvement and your skillset, all of which comes back to your passion. Do you love this brand? Is the day-to-day running of this business something that you want to succeed in?

What people don't realize in business is how many hours go into behind-the-scenes planning, admin, bookkeeping, stock-takes, and ordering—the list doesn't end! Keeping your staff happy and creating a community culture within your team can take a considerable amount of time just on its own.

All these things need to be defined from the beginning, and you need to let the franchisor know your intentions early on. There's nothing worse than promising the world to get selected, and then after week one, you decide it's not for you and you want to step back and work only one hour a week at it, or not at all.

When I first started KX, I had nothing to my name. I lived with my parents, and I was in debt, but at that time, I didn't have a family or any extensive responsibilities like a mortgage over my head. If I failed, I would have owed some money to the bank, sure, but I wasn't putting anyone else in jeopardy. I had very little to lose; whereas others have so many more responsibilities, so much more to lose. Therefore, it's essential to understand your risk profile and what you are willing to risk to succeed.

There are so many upsides to owning your own business, but it takes a lot of hard work, especially in the beginning, to succeed.

CREATING A FRANCHISE

Can Your Business be Franchised?

It's one thing to want to franchise your business; it's another thing for your business to be franchisable.

First, your business needs to make money within a franchise model, not just as a company-owned business. If you join an existing franchise, you will need to pay franchise royalties and marketing fund dollars, which will be a new expense to any existing business. Hence, no matter how much hype is around your business, that excitement means nothing if a Franchise Partner won't make their return on investment within three years (give or take).

Deciding to Franchise Your Business

First, you need to prove that your business concept works. If you can show you're profitable by the end of the initial phase (three years), you're already ahead of the seventy percent of small businesses in Australia that fail in the first three years. This also goes for any potential Franchise Partners. Whatever money they invest in starting a business under your franchise, they need to know they're likely to make it back within approximately the first 3-4 years, or else they won't bother.

The reward for going out on your own is big, but it's a lonely ride. The first eighteen months of starting KX were incredibly hard.

Ask yourself, can you commit to something, day in, day out, for ten years of hard work, constantly having to reinvest profits to grow? In one sense, ten years is a very long time, but it's also a very short amount of time to set you and your family up for life if your franchise is successful.

If you want to build something from scratch, call it your own and control every little piece of it, then owning a franchise might not be for you.

After a full day's work, when the doors close, you're stuck talking to yourself while doing the tedious tasks that a business requires you to do. So, there are pros and cons to both, which need careful consideration.

JOINING A FRANCHISE

Is Buying a Franchise Right for You?

You might be highly entrepreneurial, or you might not have any business experience. Both can be successful in a franchise—but will it be suitable for you?

Buying into a franchise means having everything at your fingertips. An established brand, website, social presence, systems, processes, support, and a collective group of like-minded people to help you. The brand has traversed the most challenging part of the journey for you, which is why franchising is so appealing. But you pay for that privilege.

Remember that it's not your company or brand you're buying into— you're licensing it and using another's system to make money. If you're okay with building an asset you will never fully own, you understand the value of a brand and the collective nature of a franchise.

Personality Matters

Consider how your personality will adapt to being in a network where you're told what you can and can't do. I was a terrible employee because I couldn't handle the restrictions of basic employment, so imagine how you might feel if you have a brilliant idea that might get knocked back for a business you own! Or perhaps you have an incredible idea that gets taken up by the franchise, but you don't get any credit or as much as you would have liked.

These are all the questions you need to ask when weighing up the positives and negatives of becoming a Franchise Partner.

From a franchisor's perspective, there is nothing better than hearing from prospective Franchise Partners about how they know that they could go and do something on their own, but they don't want to. They believe in the system, the brand, and in doing it with a team.

Understand that the brand comes first. It has to come first because if one Franchise Partner tarnishes the brand, it can affect the entire franchise network. The quicker you learn that the brand comes first and, as a Franchise Partner, your contribution is secondary to the collective, the easier it will be to enjoy the ride and succeed in your franchise.

There is nothing worse than having a Franchise Partner push back on every campaign or change the franchisor wants to implement. Ultimately, it is the franchisor's business, and they have the right to change, adapt, and move the model however they see fit. Good franchisors will listen, consult, and involve Franchise Partners during the process, but others won't, so you need to understand the relationship and that all of these scenarios can occur. You might disagree with a decision, but the ability to accept, understand, and move forward with the franchisor will enable you to succeed in a franchise model.

The Recruitment Process

The recruiting process to become a Franchise Partner is very similar to a job interview, and the best candidates will do their research before applying. There is nothing more impressive than sitting down with a potential Franchise Partner, and they know everything to do with your brand: from the founders and executive team to the history and the brand values.

If you're a current client or customer of the franchise business, which is often the case, talk to that franchise owner. Most will happily sit down for coffee with you and tell you about their journey as a Franchise Partner, how they got to do what they currently do, and reveal how the relationship is with the franchisor once the papers are signed, and the business is running. Use the opportunity to find out about the day-to-day operations, how many hours they give back to the business a week, and how that has changed over time.

If you can live the life of a current Franchise Partner, it will give you the best picture of whether franchising—or this franchise in particular—is right for you. How do you know you will love the day-to-day of this business unless you experience it for yourself? Being a client or customer of a business is very different from working in it. It's an entirely different dynamic. If you can shadow a current Franchise Partner for a week, you can use the opportunity to get a feel for the business at different times of the day and different days of the week. Observe the various dynamics of the business throughout an extended period so there are no surprises when you finally open your doors.

Consider also how you found the recruitment process. Was the recruiter responsive? Do you feel like the franchisor cares about you, or are they just after another sale? Talking to other owners in the network to find out the true nature of the relationship between franchisor and Franchise Partner should be part of your due diligence.

The recruitment process is also a clear indication of how the system and the processes work in the franchise. A professionally run, organized recruitment process that manages your expectations and sets out the steps of the procedure is a good indication that the franchise is well run.

> *There is a symbiotic relationship between the franchisor and Franchise Partner: you cannot succeed unless they succeed.*

Just as teams need a league, they also need rules, regulations, coaches, and referees in order to play and succeed to the best of their ability. Likewise, a franchise needs all of its critical parts and people to succeed. This is the single most crucial point when it comes to the Franchise Partner and franchisor relationship.

What to Look for in a Franchisor

Business partnerships are often considered "commercial marriages." In a franchise situation, you need to understand that you are entering a commercial marriage with someone who has more control than you do. Both parties need to respect, trust, and be loyal to one another. They need to do right by one another, but the franchisor has the final say. Do you feel comfortable with the franchisor having that much power?

If the answer is "yes," you're ready to delve further into the Franchise Agreement and Disclosure Document. It's imperative that, when you receive these documents, you read them thoroughly and understand them fully. Write down as many questions as possible, so when your legal team reviews the documents, you can fully understand the expected relationship.

The ultimate test is trust. When you're talking to the franchisor, do you trust them? They will be in a position to make decisions that affect your business and your livelihood. It comes down to expectations, aligning theirs with yours, or at least putting everything on the table, so there are no surprises.

Remember, always go with your gut. Trust that little voice in your head. If you think, "Oh, I'm not happy with that, but we could work it out," it will likely hurt you in the end.

Relationships tend to break down when one thing is said, and another is actioned. As soon as trust is broken in a Franchise Partner/franchisor relationship, it is hard to reclaim.

Talk to other owners in the network. It's an excellent opportunity to find out how the franchisor conducts themselves in business to evaluate whether you can start and maintain a business relationship with them.

Spend some time understanding the Franchise Code of Conduct relevant to your country or region. Australia is the most regulated country in the world when it comes to franchising, and its code holds all the things that franchisors can and can't do. Reading the code gives you a complete understanding of the obligations of both the franchisor and Franchise Partner. Nothing is hidden, and there is no excuse for not knowing.

After you've worked through all these documents and agreed to them, put the paperwork in the bottom drawer. A good franchisor will be able to sort out any issues without them. Trust and communication are so important. It's when you need to take them out again that you know the relationship is in question.

What Franchisors Expect

The relationship should start with mutual respect and an understanding to strengthen communication between the franchisor and Franchise Partner. Trust is everything. Franchisors need to trust that the Franchise Partner will do the right thing by the brand, and the Franchise Partner needs to trust that the franchisor will do the right thing by the Franchise Partner.

The most successful Franchise Partners in our network share similar character traits.

1. They take full responsibility.

First of all, they take full responsibility for their own business. They have mastered the system, know the ins and outs of the business, have studied the operations manuals like textbooks, and rarely ask for our help unless they really need it or can't find it anywhere else. These Franchise Partners build a culture that makes their team feel connected, locally and to the larger brand. As an owner, it is up to you to look after your team members. How will you incentivize them? What training and learning will you offer? How are they going to grow and develop? How will you portray the company culture within your team?

2. They know their business inside out.
Successful Franchise Partners know their numbers. They're across the reporting, and they know what is happening in their business. They understand why they had a bad month and plan to improve it next month. They come to business performance management meetings ready to listen, share their insights, and take on feedback.

3. They give above and beyond customer service.
They make sure clients are treated exceptionally well. The mentality of making sure the business does everything within its power to please the client and make them feel a part of the community is powerful. This ranges from sending flowers to clients getting married, giving recognition to loyal clients, or impressing for no other reason than just because they can. They send thank you cards for no reason except to say thank you.

4. They build local connections.
While franchisors control the bigger picture, Franchise Partners do a lot at a local level. Our most successful Franchise Partners connect with their local business community, networking with their neighbors to promote and support each other. This might be as simple as being a regular at a local hair salon or café, forming strategic partnerships, and joining community business groups. The more you give back to the community, the more it will give back to you and your business.

All of these things collectively make a great Franchise Partner. For KX, these traits align with the KX core values. Our Franchise Partners embody these behaviors every single day. It's not a coincidence that they are the best performers in our network.

Yes, they question franchisor decisions, but they trust and understand what business they are in, and they adapt, accept change quickly, and move forward. Overall, the best indication that they want to succeed alongside you is that they're advocates of the brand.

THE (HARMONIOUS) FRANCHISE RELATIONSHIP

At KX, it's easy to talk about respectful relationships because it's our first company value. In a franchise network, the Franchise Partner and franchisor must work together and form a good relationship.

Communication is the key to building a good relationship, so consider the lines of communication throughout the network. In a smaller franchise, you might have direct contact with the founder or CEO. However, in most cases, you'll be in touch with a business development manager or business performance manager.

The ratio of franchises per manager is important. Up to thirty stores per manager is generally a good indication that the franchise provides solid support for its network; whereas one hundred stores per manager is unlikely to give you a ready line of communication or have someone available when you need them.

However, if the ratio is high, it may be that their processes and systems are streamlined and easy to follow, so they don't need to provide as much support. This may be the case with franchises that invest very heavily in getting all their systems, process, and operations manuals updated, correct, and extremely detailed, so it is rare you would have to contact someone for help.

Evaluating communication lines will give you a good indication of how things will go for you in your very early days. You will need the most support in the first twelve months of operating your business, and you need to know what level of support and information the franchisor offers to give you the highest chances of success.

If you currently own a franchise, the franchise relationship is already established, and it takes work on both sides to maintain it. It's common for a franchisor never to hear when things are going well, only when things haven't worked out as planned, so make sure you're communicating well throughout.

MAKING THE DECISION

Although buying a franchise means the franchisor will give you all the tools, systems, marketing material, and operations support you need to run a business, understand that in the end, it's your business and you're responsible for its success or failure. While franchises have better odds of succeeding than other stand-alone businesses, they can still fail, which is outside the franchisor's remit.

As much as franchisors can hold your hand as you go from step to step in the system, there may be other factors outside their control where you will need to rely on your initiative to find solutions for your business.

In my experience as a franchisor, the hardest working Franchise Partners have been the most successful. They take the initiative to learn from people in other areas about different businesses and improve themselves, their businesses, their team, their culture, and their systems and processes to succeed at the highest level.

At the 2019 KX Conference, guest speaker Paul Brown said something that stuck with me:

"Don't comment on the system until you are an expert at the system."

As a Franchise Partner, you need to follow the system to understand why things are the way they are. The key to a good franchise relationship is asking questions, and for the franchisor to be comfortable explaining the answers.

If you don't understand a day in the life of a franchisor, ask questions or spend a day in the head office to see how all the wheels turn. You'll soon realize how much hard work goes on behind the scenes. Most of the time, a franchisor has done what the Franchise Partner is doing to run a store or studio. Often, they know what you're going through, and they respect that you might struggle with some decisions. It comes down to that respectful relationship.

NEVER STOP LEARNING

From a learning and development perspective, look at the Certified Franchise Executive (CFE) program run by the International Franchise Association (IFA) in the USA. The FCA facilitates the course (IFA counterpart) in Australia. For more information: https://www.franchise.org.au/education/cfe-program/

The FCA gives you certification to show that you're learning as much as you can about franchising and works on the accrual of points from certain learning events and conferences. It also shows you're serious about the franchise industry and the long-term success of your franchise.

LEAVING THE FRANCHISE

Franchising is not for everyone. If you've had a go and found you're not suited to playing by someone else's rules, or if you want the challenge of making it on your own, then stop wasting your time fighting a franchisor. There is no courage in believing that you can do better and not going out and doing it. I'm not here to talk you out of it; I'm here to talk to you into it.

You might not want to sell your business now, but I recommend putting it in a saleable position as soon as you can. A typical sale takes between 6–12 months, and the best time to sell is when you don't have to, so it's good to be prepared in advance.

Business brokers will often have industry benchmarks on your business's sale value. The fitness industry hovers around 2.5–3 x EBIT (earnings before interest and taxes).

There's nothing worse than being desperate. If you have even an inkling of wanting to sell, start the process at least twelve months before you want out.

Before you sell, clean up your books. You need two years of solid financials, which includes taking all of the irrelevant expenses out, so the modeling is clean. Then you must put feelers out while maintaining business performance. In my experience, more often than not, when someone wants to sell, their mind leaves their business; performance drops, and declining revenue and profit shortly follow. This will only hurt your sale price, as the buyer will not buy what the business *was*. They will buy what the business currently *is*—there is no value in "potential" or "how it used to perform."

Lastly, be aware of your legacy. The buyer needs to be a good fit for the franchise, so don't waste the franchisor's time if you know they don't hold the company's values. Just because they are waving money in your face does not mean the franchisor will accept that they'll be the next Franchise Partner of your business.

STORIES OF SPIRIT, PASSION, AND SUCCESS FROM OUR FRANCHISE PARTNERS

It's easy for me to talk about the Franchise Partner/franchisor relationship as I have lived and breathed it for over ten years, but my experience is as a franchisor. So, I thought it fitting to include advice from our Franchise Partners about being involved in a franchise.

Eli Censor

@elicensor

You would recall earlier that Eli was my first follower. She joined the business when it was barely known, and if there was a Franchise Partner who has seen the most change in this company, it would be Eli.

Eli's words of wisdom:

> My one piece of advice would be to meet as many existing owners and head office staff as possible before signing on. You can really get an idea of the culture of the company and the way things work by chatting to people already in the network. It's all about the people involved.
>
> I attest my success to growing an exceptional team around me. There is no way I could have grown my group without the amazing people that surround me who have come along for the journey. Finding stand-out employees early on that I then created business opportunities for, and getting their long term buy-in together, has made us all successful.

Angella [Ange] Kounelis

@ange_kouns

So, you now know the story of Eli Censor and her contribution to the company. Well, here's some more proof that this company has always been based around relationships.

I met Ange through Eli. With the fantastic initial success of the Richmond (VIC) studio in 2012, Eli, as the studio and brand ambassador, was screaming to all her connections about just how amazing KX was. Ange, being Eli's training buddy, was one of the people who got the message. Ange had been a personal trainer for two years and was amazing at connecting with people. Before her fitness career, she was an air hostess for four years, living abroad in the Middle East, so her customer service and relationship skills were incredible.

After suffering from self-esteem issues and navigating through an eating disorder in her twenties, Ange has this incredible gift of understanding similar difficulties that her clients, especially women, are experiencing. She could relate, understand, empathize, and then support and coach in such a comforting way that she got her clients results and retained them long-term. She became their sidekick that they could not live without. Although Ange was a fantastic personal trainer, she got a bit stale on the pretentious gym environment and was looking for a change.

With Ange, ever since we met, it has always been an open and honest relationship. I can still remember the café where I met her for the first time, and, question after question, she dug deep into all business assets. She asked about how we were going to do some things, and I just didn't know the answer, so I openly turned to her and said, "To be honest, I have no idea just yet, but what I do know is that together we'll figure it out."

When explaining why she signed on as one of my first Franchise Partners in 2013, Ange attests to that raw, open, and honest conversation and connection. Her Glen Waverley (VIC) studio was an instant success, and it was a true testament to Ange's hard work and dedication to her studio and her community. Over the years, she has added three more studios to her portfolio (total four) in Victoria. She is one of our most loved and respected Franchise Partners across the entire network and was also a resident trainer on our Bali retreats every year. Ange lives and breathes the KX values, and her success has been so remarkable to witness.

Ange's words of wisdom:

> My one piece of advice is to do it! If the passion is real and keeps coming up for you, follow your dreams and go for it. It's obviously hard work, but the relationships, self-growth, and community you can build are truly magical. Franchising means you have a community of other owners to grow with and learn from, so be sure to ask questions and seek advice. We have all been where you are!
>
> I attribute my success to my passion. I'm passionate about the product, the people, and the brand. I lead from the heart and believe in providing an exceptional customer service experience for all my clients. I also work very hard on my mental health, which to me is just as important as my physical health in business. If I show up and be present for my team, my community grows, and I can continue to succeed personally and professionally. My favorite business tool I learned many years ago was to be resilient and persevere. As Angela Duckworth says, "Enthusiasm is common. Endurance is rare." So let's just say, I keep going…

Ange Kounelis

Jess Rowlands

@kxpilateschelsea

Jess is another of our amazing Franchise Partners. She started off as a Trainer but after two years of teaching at KX, the opportunity to open her own studio in Chelsea (VIC) came up, and she jumped on it.

Initially, Jess thought she was going to be a police officer. She even took two years of legal practice studies after high school but never quite felt ready to join the police force. She worked as a legal secretary for five years and during that time, she decided that being a police officer wasn't for her. The shift work alone wasn't compatible with her plans to start a family one day.

With a love for all things sport and fitness—especially calisthenics—the "become a personal trainer" ads she heard on the radio every day on the way to her stressful office job didn't take long to convince her to do just that.

After completing her PT course, Jess scored a position as floor manager at a new local gym, gained some clients, and expanded her expertise to become a mat and reformer Pilates instructor.

Due to her calisthenics experience, which involved performing on stage, she was—and still is!—a natural at taking group fitness classes. She worked as a PT and group fitness instructor for ten years before she was drawn to KX.

Jess's words of wisdom:

> I had always done Pilates on the mat as part of my calis-
> thenics practice. I first experienced reformer Pilates due to
> a hamstring injury when I was about twelve years old and
> used it for rehab purposes. The Pilates mat and reformer
> movements did wonders to heal my torn hamstring. I decided
> to take up the Pilates course, as it was a movement I had
> known, believed in, and loved almost my entire life. Not

only for its healing purpose, but the workout it gave. It was something I could teach to people long-term that wasn't going to wreck my body teaching every day of the week. Pilates is so inclusive and suitable for all ages and fitness levels.

I found out about KX via good ol' Groupon (group voucher company), and I discovered a few studios around Melbourne. One morning when I was training a client at the gym, she asked me if I had heard of KX and if I would be interested in working at a new studio opening in the area. At that time, I was also running boot camps for a small company on top of my gym work, so I really didn't have any spare time. However, it actually sounded like a really good opportunity to change it up plus work in a warm, modern, boutique studio rather than cold, run-down scout halls!

When the opportunity to open my own studio in Chelsea arose, as a Trainer, I was traveling a fair bit to and from work and working the early starts and late nights, so the thought of having my own space down the road from home was a no brainer. I was ready for the next step and had the support of my husband and family. I honestly didn't think too much about it; I just did it and trusted the process. I trusted the brand. I knew it was the next step for me.

If you're going to buy a franchise or start a business, have a solid support team. Whether it be a family or friends or a team of people who will be working with you to have your back and listen to your plans, or sometimes you just need someone to vent to so you don't feel alone. I love being a franchisee of this brand that I've been a part of for so many years and know it inside and out. The support I got from day one has been a godsend, from studio setup to ongoing monthly catch ups. I could not have done this on my own and would not want to.

I strongly believe being a KX Trainer prior to being a Franchise Partner is a huge advantage. I was teaching six days a week upon opening the studio (which is crazy); however, I got to meet so many clients and start building strong relationships. Prior to having my first baby, I was teaching at least three days per week, then was around the studio on other days, being present and connect-

Jess Rowlands

ing with the clients and being there for the staff. Being the face of the business and being present is such a huge factor.

I have created a culture amongst my team/business that is fully inclusive and a level playing field. I may be the owner, and we have more experienced trainers than others, but everyone is treated on a level playing ground, and no one is more superior than the other. Same applies for the clients. Our most experienced client will get the same treatment as a client on their first class. I want to empower and support the new team members and clients coming through and ensure they are not intimidated. I want them to feel encouraged in a supportive workplace/ studio. It's important for me to ensure my team and clients love coming to the studio, so I create a space that is enjoyable to come to, knowing I have their backs anytime they need.

My "why" is my staff and my clients. People rely on me. People get out of bed at 5 am to come to Pilates, so we can't let them down. My staff need and want their jobs. To support my staff and look after my clients is why I'm doing this job. I have been in this industry for so long because nothing makes me happier than when I or my team can make an impact on people's lives, no matter how big or small. Nothing brings me more joy than changing lives for the better, especially with a side of smiles and laughs in the process. To have fun at work makes it not feel like work at all. It is never a drag or a chore. I would never go back to the corporate world where you count down the hours till home time.

KX Chelsea opened in 2017, and I took over KX Mentone with my business partner Simone in 2022. I am continuously learning, growing, and improving, and I can't see that stopping anytime soon. As much as the fitness industry is competitive, I compete against myself and focus on how I can improve on a professional and personal level. I don't worry about what's going on around me. I focus on my own growth.

Mike Li and Jessie Zhang
@kxpilatesparramatta

Mike and Jessie have always loved fitness and trying new modalities in the fitness world. Jessie traveled all over Sydney and globally, trying all of the latest offerings, including yoga, Pilates, Barry's Bootcamp, F45, and whatever other new trends she could find. During this time, she developed a real passion for Pilates, and it was something she always stuck with. Even on their European honeymoon, Jessie would book classes at different Pilates studios in Germany, coming back to Mike afterwards to critique the experience.

Mike, on the other hand, was very much into sport and going to the gym. Before he was introduced to Pilates, he was playing basketball and tennis 3–4 times per week. In between playing sports, he would go to the gym. He never considered joining a boutique fitness studio. When Jessie introduced him to reformer Pilates, he assumed it was just a fad and something more aimed at females. However, he soon found that Pilates not only improved his movement in sport, but it also decreased the frequency and severity of his injuries. From that moment on, he has been a reformer Pilates enthusiast.

In 2020, Jessie decided to transition from a KX client to a Trainer at the Balmain (NSW) studio in Sydney, and it wasn't long before she and Mike were ready to take the next step and become KX Franchise Partners.

Mike's words of wisdom:

On a professional level, Jessie has a background in exercise physiology, and her work in rehab for the older and injured population really influenced her love for Pilates. She has a diploma of Pilates from Pilates ITC (PITC), which is a government-accredited qualification. Jessie discovered KX back in 2015, and she knew it was the right mix of traditional Pilates philosophy and a modern, high-intensity workout that she wanted to be a part of.

In 2017, we explored franchising KX. We attended the franchising expo and spoke with KX representatives, but we decided to move overseas and parked the KX idea. Whilst in China, Jessie opened her own independent boutique Pilates studio in the Beijing expat district and serviced locals and expats alike. In early 2020, we decided to move back to Sydney, and we once again explored becoming a KX Franchise Partner.

My background is in financial services. I worked at AMP Capital in the funds management investment teams for over nine years before moving to China to help drive international investments for a large retail conglomerate. My experience was more in understanding businesses and the operational side of things. But my love for fitness was always there, even in corporate. Looking back now, I was always helping to organize lunchtime or before-work boot camps for colleagues. I was heavily involved in the fitness community at AMP as well as fitness charity and fundraising events. I participated in corporate games every year and was down at the AMP gym almost every day.

As a KX client, Jessie knew that successful studios all have amazing Trainers, so she wanted to be a KX Trainer before becoming a Franchise Partner. At the Balmain studio, one of the original Franchise Partners in NSW took her under his wing. With KX Balmain's mature clientele, Jessie had to quickly improve and deliver high-quality classes for existing clients, who were used to a very high standard.

When we were ready, we finally began the process of becoming Franchise Partners, opening our first studio in Parramatta (NSW) in June of 2021 and our second studio in Thornleigh (NSW) in August of 2022. If you're thinking about becoming a franchisee, it's important to find a brand that resonates with you. You should speak with the management team to understand the vision for the company and whether it aligns with your values. The more we learned about KX, the more we knew we were the perfect fit.

Jessie and I both love the genuine interactions we have with clients, and seeing the benefits that our clients experience both physically and mentally gives us a lot of joy. We're very real in our communities, and we're inclusive and welcoming of those who may be new to reformer Pilates. This is a big part of our success. But,

Mike Li and Jessie Zhang

to us, success is about more than just being the best at one thing. It's about doing many little things well. Consistency is an overarching factor in our success, whether it's consistency in delivering high-quality classes, consistency of customer service and communication, or consistency of our scheduling. Clients know they can rely on us. With almost no class cancellations for a whole year, we have built a deep trust with our community.

We believe that team culture is influenced top-down. We aim to be transparent, considerate, and passionate ourselves so our team can also exhibit these similar values to our clients. We aim to be transparent through continuous open communication with the team and holding in-studio workshops for team bonding and improvement. We celebrate the wins, but we also acknowledge areas where we need to improve.

Everyone in the team has a voice, and we welcome feedback and suggestions. At a workshop in 2022, we practiced giving each other feedback, including raw, constructive feedback. We believe it is important to be able to accept not just the good things we do but also what we can look to improve on.

We aim to be considerate and inclusive by surrounding ourselves with a team that is diverse and open to different values and cultures. As a team, we should be relatable to our client base.

We aim to be passionate about health and fitness by being the biggest ambassadors for movement, and we get excited about delivering the highest quality classes so our clients are getting stronger every day. We love sharing class flows with each other so that we are always delivering the highest quality classes, and this passion for Pilates comes across to our clients very clearly.

EXITING A FRANCHISE

I am often asked what my exit plan is, and, to be honest, I never really know. Not yet, anyway.

Initially, in the early years of KX, I wrote down on a piece of paper, "fifty franchises, ten company studios, and then sell." After reaching this milestone in 2019, and with the international expansion taking place, there is so much more to be done and so many places to take the KX experience. I question what we would do if we sold KX. I don't think I'd want to go back to a startup to grind out the first 1–4 years again.

Until mine and Andi's passion shifts, IF that day ever comes, KX just seems so ingrained in us that it is very hard to even think of letting it go. It may be cliché, but we can honestly say, "We have never worked a day in our lives."

EPILOGUE

"Thank you to the real risk-takers, who trusted a simple guy with a big vision."

—Aaron Smith

TAKE RISKS. SEARCH FOR FREEDOM, AND YOU'LL FIND ADVENTURE

I love being the founder. I love the relationships I have built with our Staff, Trainers, Suppliers, and Franchise Partners. I love being involved in the innovation, international development, and KX brand direction. I love seeing the look on a Franchise Partner's face when they open the doors to their very own KX Pilates studio (or second, or fifth! No matter the number, it's still the same). I love seeing clients' faces when they leave a KX studio, exhausted but smiling and satisfied. I love knowing that no matter what role someone has in this company, whether a Franchise Partner, Trainer, or HQ staff member, the KX team runs through the door to work every morning, feeling fulfilled and loving their work. And I especially love the reactions from people in the street when they see the KX logo on my shirt and tell me which studio they go to and how much they love the brand.

Until that love and affection for this brand leave me, I'll be involved for a long time to come.

When I look back over a decade of our hard work and success, I feel so grateful.

To the courageous people who risked a lot, so KX could succeed.

To those who took a chance on a startup, not even knowing if any of this was going to work.

To those who moved their lives from other countries, seeking an opportunity with KX.

To those who uprooted their lives to move interstate or internationally for a brand not yet known there.

To those who quit corporate careers to follow their dream of owning their own business, choosing lifestyle and their passion for fitness over dollars.

To those who left higher-paying roles with more prominent companies, sacrificing more security to come and work for us.

To my parents, who provided their signatures, endless support, and financial backing, taking a risk on nothing more than their son's vision and the belief they had in me.

To my gorgeous wife Andi, who risked it all on a twenty-six-year-old guy who had no money, lived with his parents, and drove his dad's car!

To everyone who has been a part of the KX Pilates journey—*thank you!*

Yes, I risked a lot on a new style of fitness in a premature boutique industry that was still in its infancy, but it was easier for me: no mortgage, no kids, no school fees, no responsibility in the world.

In many ways, so many people who are now ingrained in KX have taken more risks than I ever did. I thank them all for their courage, and I am so proud to have them as a part of our family.

Business is about relationships, passion, hard work, and enjoying the journey.

So, What's Next?

I am so proud of where we have come from: a single studio where not a single person walked in on the first day to being on track to reach 150 studios nationally by 2027 and 500 studios globally by 2030. I am even more excited for where we will go next. KX has been a vehicle for me to live out my two personal values of adventure and freedom. To know that, each day, the KX team makes people's bodies stronger and lives better is an extremely satisfying feeling.

For me, KX feels like my first child.

As the business matures, so does my role in it. Stepping down as CEO was the first move into the next phase of my business life where I will focus on equipment innovation and international expansion. But in 2020, with COVID-19 putting our business on its knees, it was apparent that the culture of KX needed assistance to get it back to where it once was. It's hard enough maintaining great culture in a growing franchise without a global pandemic closing the doors of most of your businesses for weeks at a time!

With my partners in China doing well on their own, requiring little assistance from Australia, and the BB-KXF now complete, the timing is great.

So, being the Founder of KX Pilates and everything that comes with it is more satisfying for me than most would know.

TESTIMONIALS FROM SOME VERY SPECIAL PEOPLE—OUR KX CLIENTS!

Without our awesome clients, KX would have no reason to exist. The people who walk through our doors are a part of the KX family, and we value the strong communities we've built around our studios. I always love a good success story, and our clients have some of the best.

How has KX Changed Your Life for the Better?

@lucyycarpenter

"I used to struggle to even leave the house and I felt exhausted and anxious all the time. Starting KX with my bff has absolutely changed my life! I love the trainers at the Brighton SA studio and I look forward to my classes every week! I've been going for over 2 years now and it's improved my physical and mental health so much and I can't wait to not be a student so I can do more classes. Thanks @kxpilatesbrightonsa team!"

@claireellen249

"I suffered a hip impingement in 2020 from having to teach in remote learning and sitting all the time. I would lie awake at night in pain and cry myself to sleep, I could hardly get through the day it hurt so much. I started KX January 2021 and have now done over 100 classes. I've gone from having to see a physio twice a week to only seeing her every two months for a check in. KX has truly changed my life @kxpilatescroydon."

@kichelle_leigh
"KX has made me stronger, healthier and happier. During every class, my mind is clear and the only thing that matters is myself in that present moment—it's the only time I feel like I can be myself without judgment, embarrassment or fear."

@miss_vlachoulis
"KX makes me want to get out of bed and start my day, even on the days when I want to hide from all life's problems. There is nothing more powerful for the mind and body than feeling present and grounded during a KX class—it's my natural stress reliever and clears my head, which helps me be a better partner, working professional and person. So grateful."

@zoecannan
"KX has helped me lose 15 kg over the last year and a bit. It's helped me become stronger and healthier and given me a bit of confidence back. Forever grateful for my best friend talking me into coming to my first class."

@mishiette
"I had quit and refused to return to a gym after I was body shamed for being a young girl with defined arms and legs. I was told that I should be slim and lean instead of having defined and strong body parts. I have struggled with being a chunky short girl all my life. The more weight I carried, the more I seemed to be chunky. For years after this, I tried to stay active in my own home with equipment and walks, but this wasn't enough. I walked into KX M-City just over a year ago with no set goal, other than to tone up my loose bits. A year on, I have become fitter, better, stronger and healthier than I could have imagined. I have been able to push my body to limits I didn't

even know existed. Thank you to the team of trainers at @kxpilatesmcity-monash for being a part of this work in progress. Without the trainers and the community at KX M-City, I would not be the person I am today."

@megan_pirouc
"I had completely lost interest in exercise and said to many 'I will never join a gym or fitness group again.' I knew that I never got any results from going so it was pointless. Then a friend invited me along to KX and from that first session I knew this was the place for me, I'd searched and searched for that feeling everyone who was gym obsessed seems to have and could never feel the same until I started at KX. I've done 52 classes now and couldn't be more obsessed with the culture, the feeling and the overall experience. Just this week I've moved to the 4kg dumbbells as well as being on intermediate springs and I feel such strength within. Thank you KX."

@kareen_j
"Heading to the studio is my mental break from the day. I love the intense burn, the new exercises and feeling of accomplishment afterwards. After a long recovery from knee surgery and basically learning to walk again about 5 years ago, I've finally built up enough muscle over the past few years to really push myself and feel strong. I'm addicted!"

@naomi.roberts81
"For someone who absolutely HATES exercise and has tried EVERYTHING, KX has made me feel I am doing something for me that is enjoyable and healthy. I don't feel it is exercise or something 'I have to do' but instead something I want to do. I enjoy walking through the KX doors knowing how I will feel walking out."

@frostygirl01
"As a psychologist I know how important exercise is for my clients' mental

health. In helping others all day we can sometimes forget about practicing what we preach! Through these most recent times in particular KX has been my go-to to ensure that for 50 minutes a few times a week I am making sure I am topping up my own tank in a safe environment."

@lizkg
"The KX team @kxpilatesbraddon and now @kxpilateskingston have been a key part of my life changing health and wellness journey over the past 2 years. I have lost 80kgs and changed my world. Shane and her team provide a safe, inclusive, happy environment for people at all stages of their journey. It was so important for me to feel like the team was walking my journey with me. KX has of course been important in my body transformation—today I am strong, fit, happy and ready to smash my next goals."

If you are still reading—thank you.
I love sharing the KX experience and hope to continue to
inspire others. If you want some more nuggets of wisdom
on franchising or fitness, I'd love to hear from you.

LinkedIn
www.linkedin.com/in/aaronsmithkx
www.linkedin.com/company/kx-pilates

Instagram @kxpilates
www.instagram.com/kxpilates
www.instagram.com/@ajs_kx

Facebook @kxpilates
www.facebook.com/kxpilates

Bonus Content
www.kxpilates.com/defineyourself-bonus

ABOUT THE AUTHOR

Founder of KX Pilates, Aaron Smith, is an award-winning fitness innovator and entrepreneur. Based on the Japanese philosophy of kaizen (continuous improvement), KX Pilates is a dynamic workout that has transformed both fitness participants and the business at large. Aaron founded KX Pilates in February 2010 and has since built it into Australia's largest Pilates franchise, with 100+ studios and growing across Australia, New Zealand, China, and Southeast Asia.

Kaizen drives Aaron physically and mentally and imbues everything he does, from the way he sharpens his business skills to the lessons he has applied to his life thus far. He lives and acts by the principle of creating a culture of empowerment for Franchise Partners so that everyone in the KX Pilates business rises with the brand's success.

In November 2018, Aaron stepped down as CEO to focus on culture, innovation, and international expansion.

As the founder of KX Pilates, he has earnt multiple awards and much recognition, including being recognized as an influential Victorian to watch by the *Herald Sun* in 2020, Australian Young Fitness Entrepreneur of the Year in 2019, named in the top three of Australia's Top 30 Franchise Executives

(2020), featured in the 2019 Top 10 Dynamic Entrepreneurs by Dynamic Business Magazine, and *The Courier Mail's* Top 20 under 40 Entrepreneurs of 2022.

He lives in the Sunshine Coast, QLD, Australia, and is married to wife and business partner, Andi Fiorenza. They have three beautiful children: Archer, Ava, and Amelia (Millie). Or collectively known as the "A-Team."

KX Pilates is always looking for the next amazing Franchise Partner to join our KX family. For franchise enquiries please visit www.kxpilates.com.au/own-a-studio.

ENDNOTES

1   Schwarzenegger, Arnold. 2012. *The New Encyclopedia of Modern Bodybuilding: The Bible of Bodybuilding, Fully Updated and Revised.* Simon and Schuster.

2   Robinson, Kara Mayer. "Pilates." WebMD. April 22, 2001. https://www.webmd.com/fitness-exercise/a-z/what-is-pilates.

3   Ogle, Marguerite. "Biography of Joseph Pilates, Exercise Pioneer." Verywell Fit. December 30, 2020. https://www.verywellfit.com/joseph-pilates-founder-of-the-pilates-method-2704455.

4   Balanced Body. "The Benefits of Pilates." Accessed May 6, 2022. https://www.pilates.com/pilates/benefits-of-pilates.

5   Stanley, Lawrence. "Trademark Lawsuit." Balanced Body. Accessed May 6, 2022. https://www.pilates.com/pilates/origins/trademark-lawsuit.

6   Business.gov.au. "Contractor Rights & Protections." Last modified June 24, 2020. https://business.gov.au/people/contractors/contractor-rights-and-protections.

7   Collins, Jim. 2001. "Good to Great." Accessed July 27, 2022. https://www.jimcollins.com/article_topics/articles/good-to-great.html.

www.ingramcontent.com/pod-product-compliance
Lightning Source LLC
Chambersburg PA
CBHW052017030426

42335CB00026B/3180